FLOWER A. NEWHOUSE

DR. STEPHEN ISAAC

TOUCHED BY ANGELS

HOW ANGELS INFLUENCE OUR DAILY LIFE

FLOWER A. NEWHOUSE
DR. STEPHEN ISAAC

TOUCHED BY ANGELS

HOW ANGELS INFLUENCE OUR DAILY LIFE

Bluestar
Communications®

Woodside, California

© 1998 Christward Ministry, Escondido, California

Published by:
Bluestar Communications
44 Bear Glenn
Woodside, CA 94062
Tel: 800-6-Bluestar

Edited by Evelyn Alemanni
Cover Art by Melhuish Strudwick
Cover design: Annette Wagner
Layout: Petra Michel

Illustrations:

In the Presence by Ann Rothan, Sisters, Oregon
Administer of Love by Ann Rothan, Sisters, Oregon
Angel by John Melhuish Strudwick, Roy Miles Gallery, London
Bridgeman Art Library Int'l Ltd., London/New York
The Angel of Death by Evelyn de Morgan, The de Morgan Foundation, London
Bridgeman Art Library Int'l Ltd., London/New York
Angel by Sir Edward Burne-Jones, Private Collection
Bridgeman Art Library Int'l Ltd., London/New York
Christ in the Sepulchre, Guarded by Angels by William Blake (1757-1827) Victoria and Albert Museum, London/
Bridgeman Art Library Int'l Ltd., London/New York
Annunciation by Sandro Botticelli (1444/5-1510), Galleria degli Uffizi, Florence, Italy/
Bridgeman Art Library Int'l Ltd., London/New York
Night with her Train of Stars by Edward Hughes
With Courtesy of Birmingham Museum and Art Gallery, Birmingham, England
Angel of Suffering, Right Hand Angel from the St. Catherine Window,Christ Church Cathedral, Oxford, by Sir
Edwarde Burne-Jones(1833-98), 1878, Curtesy of Dean & Canons of Christ Church Cathedral, Oxford/
Bridgeman Art Library Int'l Ltd., London/New York
Twilight Fantasies by Edward Robert Hughes (1851-1914), The Maas Gallery, London/
Bridgeman Art Library Int'l Ltd., London/New York

First printing 1998
ISBN: 1-885394-31-4

Library of Congress Cataloging-in-Publication Data
Newhouse, Flower Arlene Sechler, 1909-
    Touched by angels : how angels influence our daily lives / Flower A.
Newhouse : edited by Stephen Isaac.
        p. cm.
    Includes bibliographical references and index.
    ISBN 1-885394-31-4
    1. Angels -- Miscellanea.   2. Christward Ministry. I. Isaac, Stephen,
1925-   . II. Title.
    BP605.C5N475   1998
    291.2' 15--dc21   98-9680
                                                                        CIP

Printed in USA

Acknowledgments

A book of this nature is the product of the efforts of a number of individuals who contributed to its research, word processing, editing, book design, and layout. I wish particularly to express my appreciation for the generous contributions of time and expertise of Gwen Hulbert, Evelyn Alemanni, William C. Vest, and my wife, Phyllis.

Stephen Isaac, Ph.D
Questhaven Retreat

Contents

Foreword

I shall never forget the moment when I first met Flower. I was ten years old. My mother had been searching for her true spiritual path and noticed an ad in the local newspaper announcing a lecture on Angels by someone named Flower Newhouse. She was prompted to attend and it was my great good fortune to accompany her.

The lecture hall was on the second floor of an old downtown building in Medford, Oregon. The room was not particularly large and we sat on wooden folding chairs facing the front. There were perhaps fifteen to twenty people present and, except for myself, they were all adults.

What I remember so clearly is the appearance of Flower at the room's entrance. She was dressed in white and, coming into the room, she paused for a moment, looking into the eyes of each one present as if to renew an old acquaintance. In my eyes, and I venture to say in the eyes of everyone else, she was an Angel incarnate. It is that moment that is imprinted in my memory. It remains as vivid in my mind today as when it first occurred.

Time passed; I continued growing up, and my family moved from our home in Oregon to be near Flower and Questhaven Retreat, her center, in Southern California. During the years that followed, I read her writings on Angels and listened to her many talks on this subject with a growing interest in such wonders as yet beyond my experience.

Then, while in my mid-twenties, a marvelous thing happened as I was waking up one morning. There was no crisis in my life. I was laying in bed with nothing particular on my mind, when suddenly I looked up into the face of the most glorious being I have ever beheld. Her entire aspect was light-filled and her large, luminous eyes shone with a depth of love beyond comprehension. All the while, she was smiling with such joy that it engulfed me. From her countenance streamed a current of delightful energy that revitalized every atom of my body. There was no judgment, nor any pending condition. I gazed into her outshining eyes for perhaps a minute or two, then slowly she faded from view leaving me in quiet rapture. As I lay there contemplating the experience, I realized this was my Guardian Angel. She was telling me I was loved without reservation and she wanted to give me this visitation as a remembrance of her steadfast presence.

I have never been the same since. Along with that first glimpse of Flower when I was a boy, these two visions of Angels remain with me undiminished. Together, they underwrite the truth of all that follows.

Stephen Isaac
Questhaven Retreat

10

About the Author
Flower A. Newhouse

From the time she was a child of six, Flower Newhouse beheld Angels and nature beings as freely as most people look upon each other. Because her gift of seeing into the Inner worlds was not understood by most adults she encountered, she soon gained the wisdom to discern and address those who would appreciate her gift of clairvoyance.

As the years passed, she was invited to speak at numerous churches and truth centers around the nation, where people valued her teachings. In 1937, when she was still in her twenties, she published her experiences with Angels in a book called *Natives of Eternity*, establishing herself as a pioneer in this field of study.

She and her husband, Lawrence, went on to found their own center and life work at a place called Questhaven Retreat in Northern San Diego County, California. Here in a

wilderness preserve encompassing 640 acres of chaparral-covered hills and live oak canyons, graced by cool Pacific winds, she continued her lectures, writing, and retreats on this enchanting subject. Her fondness for these selfless, steadfast beings never faltered. Indeed, she gathered around her a number of talented artists whom she inspired over the years to capture glimpses of Angelic presences. She also celebrated annually a major three-day retreat honoring the Angels on the occasion of Michaelmas at the end of September.

Questhaven Retreat, with its Church of the Holy Quest, Friendship House, Academy and Library, and a variety of guest accommodations is a unique and consecrated center to the Lord Christ. Interested readers may contact this nature sanctuary at:

Questhaven Retreat
20560 Questhaven Road
Escondido, CA. 92029
phone: 760-744-1500
web site: www.questhaven.org

The Kingdom of Angels

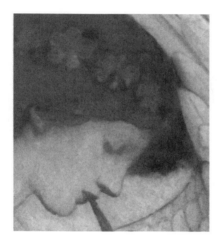

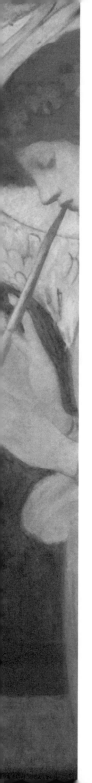

14

Our story begins in the Inner Worlds—what the Lord Christ called the Kingdom of Heaven. Here lies our true homeland as well as the abode of Angels. Here is where we reside between incarnations. And we speak in terms of worlds because there are numerous levels or dimensions that compose this kingdom. More of these glorious realms will be described as our story unfolds, but for the moment, let us just acknowledge the existence of the Inner Worlds and open the door to their exploration.

The source of the knowledge within this book is a soul who spent her life founding a work of Christian mysticism whose central theme is the experience of God, Christ, and the Inner Worlds. The purpose of this work was never to amaze its followers or glamorize the subject but, like the voyage of Columbus, to open up new realities — to challenge the "flat world" notions of conventional viewpoints and to swing wide the gates of the dormant sixth sense, which is intuition. The name of this soul was Flower A. Newhouse, and she came into her present incarnation with the ability to see clearly into the inner dimensions. What she saw were all manner of inhabitants of the Inner Worlds: nature beings, Angels, great souls who have mastered the lessons of life, magnificent realms of form and color beyond description—in a word, heaven and all its wonders.

From the past, she recalled previous lives and the harvest of insights and remembrances that summed up her wisdom as a teacher. Out of the wealth of this background, two charges were given her to unfold this lifetime: to re-ignite the flames of Christian mysticism as the foundation for living the Life and following the Way and, second, to help people rediscover the Kingdom of Angels.

It is the latter of these two commissions that this book addresses, and one Flower was uniquely gifted to fulfill. Some fourteen lives ago she exchanged her existence as an Angel to enter the human line of evolution, an uncommon step for such a being, but one with the mission of bringing the two kingdoms closer together. In making this transformation, she brought with her the clairvoyance, or inner sight, she knew as an Angel, as well as that kingdom's salient values of obedience to the Divine, honoring of truth, and selfless love.

Her kinship with the angelic line of evolution made of Flower a most remarkable revealer of their ways and forms of service. More than that, she was a fascinating person in her own right. To meet her for the first time — most often attending one of her lectures — was to behold an Angel incarnate. There was about her an authority born of her origin and experience that underscored the veracity of her words. She spoke as one who knew firsthand the truth of what she had to say. Her bearing and mannerisms reflected the grace and joy that characterizes the Angels. But the most compelling evidence of her nativity as an Angel was her steadfastness in living the Life. Daily, she went about her Father's business. She was remarkably consistent in all of life's settings, and always exemplary. She lived as she taught. There was about her no trace of hypocrisy or good intentions gone astray.

A particularly revealing aspect of Flower's awareness of the Inner Worlds came through her eyes. She was constantly surveying her surroundings for the presence of Angels and nature beings. One might be in the midst of a conversation, only to notice her eyes glancing about pleasantly, greeting the otherwise unseen visitors. When she beheld one of these celestial beings, her eyes seemed to look past anyone with her, much as someone might stare off into empty space when preoccupied with some distracting thought. Only in her case, she was seeing with the third eye, a focusing that looks beyond what the outer eyes ordinarily see. This was even more evident when she was studying an individual's aura. In the few seconds this took, she seemed to be looking through the person's entire being to something deep within.

These other worlds that Flower gazed upon are known only indirectly and intuitively to the rest of us who do not share her clairvoyant gifts. Certainly our best approximation to their reality is our innate longing for a perfect world— a world in which there is absolute truth and justice, harmony and beauty, peace and love. In our ignorance we regard such notions as idealistic and naive — a childlike fantasy of what ought to be but never is. Still, there is a compelling fascination with the thought, as though we once knew such a place and somehow we must find it again. Every great religion, one way or another, promises the existence of such a heavenly realm, be it called Paradise, Nirvana, Arcadia or Valhalla, teaching us that if we are faithful and true, it will be our destiny.

Flower taught that these Inner Worlds are indeed ideal and real and that our dim remembrance of these magnificent dominions are what keeps our hopes alive. Her descriptions of the Angel Kingdom tell of an orderly, obedient, harmonious dominion free of the passions and pains of the human path. Moreover, it is an older evolution than its human counterpart and its citizenry are vastly more advanced. Their motivation is utterly selfless and purposeful, standing in striking contrast to the underlying conflicts and self-serving inclinations with which humans struggle.

In the scheme of things, Angels play a central role in serving their Creator by being the means of maintaining the framework and order that holds the universe together. Setting aside for the moment the circumstances of Angels involved with our planet, consider the awesome sweep of the known universe—an unimaginably vast extension of space some fifteen billion light years across, and for the most part empty except for, here and there, billions of scattered galaxies, each containing billions of stars and a number of planets. It is no wonder, Flower has commented that the handful of angelic orders of which we on earth can be made aware is but a fraction of those that exist throughout the galaxies. Granted, while such a consideration far exceeds our capacity to assimilate it, it does underscore the immensity of God's reach and the vital part Angels play in the fulfillment of His design for the whole of creation.

Closer to our own lives, Angels are a significant source of influence and illumination in all that we do to further our own evolutionary unfoldment. In particular, they are the principal means of our drawing closer to God, an outcome which lies at the heart of mysticism. Unfortunately, human beings are in such a habit of assuming credit for all that comes out of our heads and hearts, we are amazingly ignorant of all that goes into these thinking and feeling functions that have their origin in the angelic realms.

Given their omnipresence and importance, it is puzzling that so little is known publicly about their reality and about their service of our planet. Certainly Angels are well recognized in the sacred books of the world's great religions. The Old and New Testaments provide clear recognition of their existence. Richer still are the books of the Apocrypha. The revelations of Mohammed were given by the Angel Gabriel. The ancient literature of India refers to beings called devas, another name for Angels. There is a whole realm of "spirits" that permeates the rise of religion from prehistoric times right up to contemporary belief systems in tribal communities.

Yet precious little is acknowledged of the nature, appearance, and purpose of Angels. They seem to manifest in an astounding manner here and there throughout the passages of history, possessing wondrous powers, only to vanish mysteriously into the silent mists. We are left with a series of isolated, unconnected incidents, giving evidence of their reality, but no clear picture of who they are, where they come from, or why they exist.

A great part of the mystery of Angels is the veil of invisibility that normally envelopes them. For most of us, what we can't see or hold in our hands tends not to exist. The few partings of this veil that have occurred provide only fragmentary glimpses of these magnificent presences. And even when we gather together all of these fragments, there are not enough pieces to form even a rough sketch of their makeup, mission, or role in the record of history. For this reason alone, it is small wonder that few people have taken them seriously.

How is this situation changing? In 1990, Sophy Burnham published her landmark volume, *A Book of Angels*. Like a draft of wind fanning long smoldering coals, the subject of Angels caught fire. Overnight, other books on this subject began to appear. Television programs, such as *Touched by an Angel*, fueled the awakening interest. What these expressions had in common was the appearance of Angels in the guise of humans, quietly and unobtrusively influencing the lives of everyday people.

Characteristic of these encounters is the sudden appearance out of nowhere of one or more friendly strangers who act to protect or awaken certain individuals with life-saving or life-changing results. When the incident is concluded, these benevolent visitors disappear as mysteriously as they arrived, never to be heard from again.

Certainly, this form of manifestation happens. A woman who attended a Michaelmas Retreat at Questhaven a few years ago told the following remarkable story. She was on her way to visit a friend in Los Angeles when, to her dismay her car suffered a flat tire. When she pulled over to the curbside intending to find a phone, several menacing gang members surrounded her car and began taunting her. Just at that moment another sedan pulled up alongside of her car. It was driven by a powerfully built black gentleman who inquired if he could be of assistance. There was about him such a commanding presence that the youths quickly found excuses to move along. He parked his car and proceeded to change her tire, all the while smiling and carrying on an engaging conversation. When he finished, he suggested another route to her friend's home and bid her safe journey. She thanked him and attempted to pay him for his services. This he graciously declined. After getting into her car, she turned one last time to wave farewell. Incredibly, there was no car or driver to be seen.

Episodes of this nature are far more common than previously realized, as the impressive number of recent books on this theme document. Just how often such incidents are truly encounters with Angels, on the one hand, or simply good Samaritans, on the other, remains unclear, but a strong case has been made for these phenomena to be authentic.

They are mentioned here because it involves appearances of Angels in a form other than their natural semblance— certainly a capability Flower has confirmed they possess.

Nevertheless, it has been Flower's lifelong endeavor to reveal Angels as they naturally appear to her clairvoyant perception and that will remain the perspective of this book. The view of the Angel Kingdom which Flower has given us to contemplate and, if possible, experience, is that of a line of evolution created by God long before the formation of its human counterpart. These extraordinary beings have been given the responsibility on a grand scale to be an extension of their Creator, maintaining order and assuring progress throughout the universe.

Concerning the planet Earth, the work of the Angels is to support the evolution and well-being of its entirety. Concerning ourselves, it is to safeguard our journey through life and mantle our drawing closer to God and all that this entails.

The chapters that follow delineate how this charge to the Angels is organized and carried out, as revealed through Flower. At the outset, it needs to be emphasized that this is a voyage of discovery. When we reach the shores of this new-found continent, the part of us that is most apt to respond first is our capacity for inner impressions and realizations. Thoughts come to us, as we say "out of the blue"—thoughts that reveal an intelligence beyond our own. These insights contain a wisdom that enriches our recognition of the Inner Worlds. They are not necessarily grand and glorious revelations worthy of a prophet but they always point out a truth about life or oneself never before grasped or appreciated. They are life-changing, transforming, enlightening moments of truth if we are wise enough to harvest them.

They most often involve the little things of our experience—the little steps of growth that, one by one, sum to a growing total.

As one who once was walking along a flower-strewn mountain trail realized: "Look, listen, and learn. All of nature teaches." What made this moment memorable was the fact that until this thought brought the hiker to a halt, his preoccupation was with the challenge of climbing to a mountain summit, all the while passing by the wonder of nature's presence and reality around and about him.

Our teacher in these moments of enlightenment, more often than not, will be our Guardian Angel. She, with infinite patience and prescience, awaits the synchronicity of circumstances that makes such revelations possible. They comprise the onset of the awakening within us of that inner perception which indeed becomes the open door to our developing selves.

We are left with one caveat. Flower often reminded her students that to receive instruction on the mysteries of life—in this instance, the Angels—is also to bear responsibility for putting this knowledge to work in our lives. To seek such information out of curiosity or intellectual acquisitiveness and not live true to its wisdom and implications, incurs a self-limiting karma in our future incarnations. Therefore, take to heart all that rings true in what follows and resolve to match the enlightenment you experience with words and deeds worthy of your revelations.

Angels of Destiny

26

Principally, four great waves, or groupings, of Angels serve our planet. One of these, the nature kingdom, is seldom directly involved with human evolution. Its legions of faithful servers range from tiny elementals which work around rocks and plants to magnificent Angel presences who govern mountain ranges, oceans, and other vast realms. These, however, are the subject of an earlier book, *The Angels of Nature.*

The three remaining groups of Angels, the focus of this book, are the Angels serving the Lord Christ, Angels serving the Holy Spirit, and Angels of Destiny. Angels serving the Lord Christ work to lift the consciousness of all humanity Godward through the ever-deepening experience of worship, healing, and prayer. Angels serving the Holy Spirit work to awaken, inspire, and enlighten individuals in all aspects of life.

The third wave, the Angels of Destiny, is the subject of this chapter. As we shall directly see, their endeavor is keyed to the progress of individuals, crafting it to the individual's karma and place on the spiritual path. It is also the wave to which our Guardian Angels belong and about whom, of all the Angel orders, we will have the most to say.

But first, to understand all three of these angelic waves supporting humanity, it is necessary to appreciate what constitutes human evolution. It has its origin in prehistoric times, much as scientists have reconstructed. In its shadowy beginnings, it is difficult to distinguish what separates the animal kingdom from the human line of evolution. But slowly the differentiating features present themselves: the development of language, the harnessing of fire, the invention of

tools, and most salient of all for its rendezvous with Angels, the appearance of religion.

Throughout these emerging practices there is this gradual unfoldment which characterizes the progress of human endeavor across the eons of time. The progress that counts the most, however, is not the collective gain for all of humanity but the individual growth that occurs as each soul surmounts a particular challenge or acquires insight into another of life's mysteries. It is in this context that the Angels become engaged with humans and are the means of bringing us to the thresholds of transformation that mark the journey Godward. Only we can exercise the will to cross over those thresholds, but it is the unfailing, deeply caring nature of Angels that sets the stage and ignites the energy that make our victories possible.

Clearly, between the beginning of the journey in primeval forests and its conclusion in the mastery of all of life's lessons at its summit, lie a multitude of lifetimes. Underlying this progression is the reality of reincarnation which makes each of our sojourns on earth a classroom in the School of Life interspersed with returns to our Homeland of Heaven, for we are indeed natives of eternity. The laws of karma governing our progress in this school, holding us accountable for our mistakes and transgressions, as well as rewarding us for our conquests and good works.

Because of the association with Eastern teachings, it is important to recognize the place of reincarnation and karma in Western thought generally and in Christian thought specifically. Reincarnation has always had a significant following throughout the Western world.

Reincarnation, by Joseph Head & S. L. Cranston, traces its origin to a legendary figure named Orpheus, founder of theology among the Greeks. This same belief in the transmigration of souls reappears in the teachings of Pythagoras, Plato, and Aristotle.

Both the Essenes and Pharisees, two of the most prominent Jewish sects in the holy land during Jesus' life, accepted this doctrine of rebirth, and it was a commonly recognized belief system throughout the world at that time. The ancient Jews were continually expecting the reincarnation of their great prophets. Even the closing words of the Old Testament illustrate this fact:

> *"Behold, I will send you Elijah the prophet before the great and terrible day of Jehovah come."* (Malachi 4:5)

Linking the Old and New Testaments, Jesus, in the book of Matthew, completes the prophecy with these salient words:

> *"Among them that are born of women there hath not risen a greater than John the Baptist ... For all the prophets and the law prophesied until John. And · if ye will receive it, this is Elias* (the Greek equivalent of 'Elijah'), *which was for to come. He that hath ears to hear, let him hear."* (Matthew 11:11-15)

In the early centuries of the Christian era, reincarnation remained a widespread belief. Origen, one of the most prominent of all the church fathers, wrote in *De Principiis* :

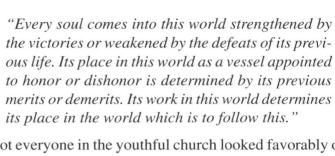

"Every soul comes into this world strengthened by the victories or weakened by the defeats of its previous life. Its place in this world as a vessel appointed to honor or dishonor is determined by its previous merits or demerits. Its work in this world determines its place in the world which is to follow this."

Not everyone in the youthful church looked favorably on the belief in reincarnation. Some perhaps because life on earth was plagued with hardships and suffering and there was little reason to want to repeat it. Far better to strive for salvation and an eternity in paradise once and for all.

Others, more focused on the future of the church itself, realized that reincarnation opened the door to procrastination about one's religious responsibilities such that members more easily could postpone commitments or obligations. How much more effective was the "now or never" position of the priests in dealing with their congregations.

In the ensuing centuries after Origen, the politics of church theologies grew more tense. So it was that this issue under the guise of pre-existence of the soul became the focus of an important church council in 553 A.D. After decades of disputes, those who supported Origen were defeated by the Byzantine Emperor Justinian and his followers. Pre-existence of the soul, and with it reincarnation, were declared anathema — that is to say, cursed and condemned. Sadly for future Christians, the doctrine of reincarnation was no longer acceptable within the church.

We need make no further mention of this history other than to say that many westerners continued to believe in the doctrine of rebirth on its own merits and that it is alive and well today. What remains important is to place this development into its historical perspective since it forms the foundation for what follows concerning the Angels of Destiny.

Coincident with the phenomenon of reincarnation is the law of karma.

To understand the role of karma, let us contrast two quite different views of life. The first viewpoint looks upon life as a series of events based solely on chance without any preordained purpose and with outcomes that have little to do with justice or fairness or merit. For such an individual, life is a combination of the luck of the draw and survival of the fittest. To be born wealthy or poor, wholebodied or handicapped, gifted or undistinguished, Eskimo or South Sea Islander, all is a matter of blind fate and sheer chance.

The second viewpoint looks upon life as absolutely purposeful, just, fair, and meritorious. All that comes to us is a product of our past choices and actions. We are the authors of our own circumstances, for better or worse, and if we would improve our lot in life, we must change who we are.

It is clear that the first instance leaves us with little control over our destiny, resulting in a cynical and resigned outlook on life. Hope is absent in our lives and we do well just to go through the motions of existence. The second instance, on the other hand, is a different story. We realize that through the exercise of our free will, we can create our own future.

Karma was briefly alluded to in Origen's quotation when he spoke of being strengthened by one's victories or weak-

ened by one's defeats. There is an even more succinct statement by the Apostle Paul:

"Whatsoever a man soweth, that shall he also reap."
(Gal. 6:7)

Both observations express the principle of karmic law which connects each of our actions with eventual consequences. In essence, karma is the accumulation both of assets we have earned and debts we have incurred.

Since we have behind us many incarnations, each containing a multiplicity of actions or inactions, for us to draw from our assets and pay our debts in preparing for our upcoming return to earth, there would need to be, in God's world, a repository of all past events affecting our karma. This repository is known by the term Akashic Records, where, as this good or bad karma builds over lifetimes, it is accurately recorded and stored. This brings us to the *Tawonel*, beings of Archangel rank, who safeguard the immense and detailed wealth of information held in the Akashic Records.

Flower describes the Akashic Records as a region in the mental plane of the Inner Worlds composed of an impressionable and highly sensitized screen of mental essence. So exacting is it that not one thought or action escapes the boundaries of our auras without becoming visible on this historical record the life of everyone who has ever lived.

Guardians of these records are the Tawonel Archangels, extraordinary beings of masculine gender who safeguard these living screens with their tremendous shields of light.

Their presence ensures that the information they protect remains accurate and uncompromised. It is also their responsibility to constantly observe the records accumulating moment by moment from all the countries of the world and from each of their citizens.

These Tawonels, Angels of Destiny, are steadfast sentinels, outshining in their inner splendor. To approach them with a request for access to these records is an awesome and intimidating encounter. Flower has said of this experience that people who ask her to investigate a past life for them have no idea of what is involved. For someone like herself it often takes hours of preparation to bring one's inner faculties to the point of readiness that will pass the muster of these Angels of Destiny. It is an exhausting task and one never to take lightly or casually. She once commented how she found herself dreading these episodes because there is such a strong likelihood that what will be found in anyone's past is not a flattering or heartwarming discovery. It is far more likely that inquiries lead to a revelation of our indiscretions, our mistakes, our failings. After all, we are looking into the past which lies behind and below us. What will be seen is less aware, less refined, more earthbound, more primitive. It is also, for the most part, remarkably uneventful and boring.

In their protective role, the Tawonel confront each inquiry of the records with four questions:

1. *Does the inquirer have integrity?*
2. *Is there a right motive prompting the question?*
3. *Will the knowledge gained be used for a good purpose and for growth?*
4. *Does the inquirer have a need to know?*

What each of these questions guards against is access to the records based on curiosity or egotism or wanting information without paying the cost—and there is always a cost. To be aware of karmic information involving past incarnations, whatever the motive, carries with it the responsibility of taking action to put wrongs aright. While the karmic debts may not necessarily be your own, at the very least you may be obligated to call unresolved matters to the attention of other persons, and this involves you in their difficulties.

Nevertheless, there can be certain occasions when perplexing problems are illuminated by events in a previous incarnation. Here's an example which illustrates how the Akashic Records helped resolve an otherwise unfathomable family dysfunction. At the age of 18, Flower had recently begun her lecturing career. She was speaking for the Theosophical Society in Hollywood, California. At the conclusion of her address, she was approached by a couple, very cultured and well-to-do, who asked for an interview the following week to address a serious domestic problem.

What the problem turned out to be was an inexplicable hatred that had developed between the father and their middle son, who was now a young adult.

As a family they had done everything they knew to understand and correct the underlying emotional confrontation—counseling, therapy, prayer — but nothing changed the deep-seated animosity. The mother, in particular, was bewildered and beside herself agonizing over the plight of her two loved ones. Could Flower shed any light on the matter?

Quietly, Flower went to the Akashic Records for insight into this perplexing dilemma. The Tawonel Archangel, confirming that the motive behind her inquiry was a worthy one, gave her entrance to the family's file. Flower found herself looking at a scene in what appeared to be a wealthy estate in Spain. She saw a man who closely resembled the father, except that his skin had a deep olive complexion. He was mounted on a white horse and in the process of giving orders to his servants. The scene then changed to a Spanish village, some distance away from the first site. The same nobleman was present in this scene. She saw him dismount and approach a very humble cottage. As he did so, the door of the cottage opened and out came a young woman who Flower immediately recognized to be the present day mother. Behind her was a young man. Flower realized that this was the middle son of the family seeking her assistance. The nobleman drew his sword and killed this youth who obviously was his rival, leaving the woman distraught and sobbing.

Other insights revealed that earlier she had been betrothed to the nobleman. But before the wedding could take place she ran off with this younger man whom she loved. Marriage to the nobleman was her family's ambition to enlarge their wealth and in no way was it her heart's desire.

After Flower's visit to the Akashic Records, she shared with the couple the karmic background that underlay the intense hatred the father and son held for each other. She explained to the father that he had been placed in this distressing position to make amends for this taking of a life. If he could now come to complete compassion and forgiveness, the relationship could be transformed. In the weeks that followed, Flower received a letter from the grateful

mother that confirmed the healing process was well underway.

Another interesting case that was illuminated by the Akashic Records involved a five-year-old boy who was brought to Flower by his parents. The child had a disturbing fixation with strangulation. While at play with other children, he would suddenly grab their throats and attempt to choke them. In the most recent incident he was caught placing a noose around another boy's neck and appeared ready to hang his playmate when the screams of the startled victim summoned help.

Beside themselves with puzzlement and fear for their son's future, the parents came to Flower for advice. When she looked at the boy, she was shown a glimpse of his previous incarnation as a Portuguese sailor. Tragically, he had been hung for a crime he had not committed. He died furiously protesting the injustice of the hanging, and this unresolved emotional trauma carried over into his present emotional body. The only outlet he had thus far found was acting out the fact that someone else should have been hung. Flower's counsel was to give the child all the love and unconditional acceptance they could, combined with wise caution and vigilance. Then, when old enough to understand, he should be informed of the origin of this obsession.

Flower has described what it is like for one with her clairvoyance to approach the Akashic Records. First of all, the ever present Tawonel Archangel presides over the event. Before her appears what seems to be a misty golden fog. Its foreground is active and lucid to a depth of what seems to be a few feet, after which it forms an impenetrable wall. She then would frame her question, and the great Angel of

Destiny instantly would either disapprove the request briefly, communicating the reason, or approve it without further comment. She would then experience an energizing of all of her inner faculties and the screen of golden fog would come alive with scenes from the past, gradually illuminating the answer.

These scenes from previous incarnations of those who were involved in the inquiry seldom explicitly identified the locale or the time period. The identity of the country or region depended on clues revealed in the scenes: the style of architecture, how people were dressed, modes of transportation, and the like. Time had to be similarly inferred, though there were often clues related to the reign of certain rulers, or the occurrence of historic events. If such information was crucial to the understanding of the situation, a glance at the Tawonel would elicit it.

What deeply impressed Flower in these episodes was the mathematical precision connecting what we have done in the past with our present fortunes or misfortunes. It left her with the clear realization that a mantle of divine justice permeates all of creation: what we sow we reap. It imbued her with a passion as a teacher to awaken in her pupils this awareness and to inspire them to make more thoughtful choices now in order to create a finer future.

As her experience with the Akashic Records grew, Flower found that it was not always necessary to go to them for an explanation of the past. For one thing, so much of our past is cluttered with our mistakes and failures that it seldom reveals an encouraging picture to share with the person seeking advice. For another, those aspects of our lives that most need attention are the direct outgrowth of these previous oversights and reappear in the present incarnation as the conditions that most challenge us. By simply recognizing these conditions as our starting points, we will be on the right track.

Moreover, Flower came to realize that her intuition was a trustworthy alternative. She had a gift of intuitive flashes, often in the form of brief glimpses into the past, that would confirm the rightness of a course of action. Take for example the case of a woman whose mother was domineering. It was clear to Flower that this was a carry-over from a one-sided relationship in the past, and it was time for the daughter to break free to establish her own independence. This insight was sufficient to address the problem and point the way for change.

The interfacing of the Akashic Records with events or conditions in our lives that reflect our karma brings us to the second great masculine order within the Angels of Destiny. This is the order of the *Kindel Archangels* who supervise human evolution through the planning and summing up of each incarnation. These resplendent beings possess intense powers of concentration, focusing minutely upon the smallest details of our lives to ensure that, in its turn, each and every karmic debt will eventually be cancelled. With equal thoroughness, they harvest the assets we have acquired and portion them out for our strategic advantage in an upcoming incarnation.

They also are endowed with a skilled use of spiritual will, an attribute that commands the attention of our souls and helps us hew to the path of progress they envision for each of us.

In many ways, the Kindel Archangels, along with our Guardian Angels, constitute the enlightened aspect of conscience that, if we pay heed, steers us through the reefs and shoals of life. Besides the cautions of conscience, they are the source of inner promptings that summon our courage and allow us to be bold adventurers on the seas of faith.

All mortal souls who incarnate come into physical existence with the major plan of their destiny carefully graphed. This process begins about a century prior to an individual's descent into the earth plane. At this time, the Kindel Angel who has charge of the complete history of an individual's entire evolution through many lives meets with a soul who requires incarnation. The Kindel and his human charge consult at length on matters concerning the needs, desires, and karmic consequences that this individual is bound to meet in the coming lifetime. When this review is finished, the Kindel slowly, painstakingly, and wisely forms what is known as the *Incarnation Disc*. Composed of mental essence, it contains numerous diagrams, each with its own destiny. One diagram will consist of all the important persons such an individual merits meeting. Another records all the high events that the individual has earned which are of life-changing significance—events of spiritual consequence with the potential to illuminate consciousness or initiate character. A third diagram contains karmic influences to be encountered in one's health, along with the duration of the coming lifetime. A fourth diagram embodies the general karmic indebtedness the individual still owes to life.

These intricate diagrams are woven into a most complex disc consisting of mental essence. The resulting Incarnation Disc possesses myriad symbols which determine patterns for the coming years—a kind of spiritual DNA. The disc is placed in the proximity of the heart region of the mental body for the duration of the coming physical life.

Through the passage of a given day, the graph's movements will bring into immediate focus various emblems on this all-important disc. Each of these is keyed to experiences, meetings, and probable conquests or disappointments that the human being will encounter.

Some of these patterns are known as *open keys*; others as *closed keys*. Open keys and closed keys invite deeper understanding for they are of great significance. The closed keys involve predestined events which the individual has incurred by actions taken or avoided in previous incarnations. They are the direct consequence of the seeds that have been sown; now the harvest must be reaped.

In most of these instances, the events take place during the same time periods in which they were met in the past. Suppose, for example, in your most recent incarnation you knew a spiritual kinship with a particular person whom you subsequently failed. What happens is that in the next life, during which you are both once again in physical incarnation at the same time, you will meet again at similar ages to repeat the tests of the past in the hope of redeeming the relationship.

Similarly, although persons do not usually undergo a testing of identical diseases, you are likely to encounter ailments of a kind similar to those you knew and failed to overcome in the past when your control was weak and ineffective.

All the while the life graph weaves a pattern conceived to be the most fitting and constructively helpful. Closed keys not only bring you the events you yet need to work on, but also the wholesome merits and gainful opportunities earned in the past. In this new incarnation, for instance, you may be entitled to improved circumstances in your home and family life such that your growing up will greatly benefit the kind of adult you will become.

Open keys are quite another matter. Unlike closed keys, which have fixed karmic components, open keys are unpatterned by one's past. Free of this influence, you are to decide afresh what new attitudes will be formed and where they will lead you. Open keys are placed within a person's life disc at every incarnation to introduce new directions, to open the door for inner changes, and to present opportunities for spiritual self-conquests. Of particular importance, they permit your Guardian Angel to consult the Kindel Angel responsible for your life planning to more wisely guide you in the choices and possibilities that lie ahead.

Nevertheless, it is impossible to predict with certainty a person's reaction to repeated tests which were formerly failed. There will come a time when that person will no longer fail, ending the cycle of the closed key which contains that lesson. This makes way for an open key and the beginning of a challenge of quite a different kind. When open keys are in focus, you have the sensation, on all planes of consciousness, of being adrift from the familiar experiences, feelings, certainties, and securities of the past. Open key periods are difficult times. They are the periods most cherished by the soul for, through them, individuals can accelerate their growth, coming to psychological maturity and spiritual enlightenment.

You may, by inner means, attune yourself to wholly new relationships, talents, and circumstances. In these periods,

no destiny affects you save that which you create through your own actions, reactions, and decisions.

For these reasons, you must pay great attention to those times when your life seems adrift. During them, concentrate on living your highest and bravest, with a strong, vital attunement to Reality. Open keys permit you to "skip grades" much like a student in a conventional school setting. They enable you to clear up more rapidly the overload of karmic indebtedness that determines the closed keys.

It is in these times, when you are not affected by the predetermined events contained in the closed keys of your Incarnation Disc, that great inner presences concerned with your progress can bring into your experience new friends, teachers, novel employments, and discoveries affording you fresh impetus and expansive vision.

With this knowledge of the Akashic Records and the Incarnation Disc, and the two great Angels of Destiny—the Tawonal and the Kindel—that work together to fashion life plans, you are now ready to begin the extraordinary adventure of incarnation itself.

The Gateway of Birth and the Awakening

44

Our time in the Inner Worlds between incarnations is a time of rest and reunion initially, followed by a careful appreciation and assimilation of lessons experienced in our most recent incarnation. Afterwards, there is an extended period of service intermingled with instruction and experiences of renewal up until the time for us to prepare once more for our return to the School of Life. It is the way of human evolution that, while we can prepare for new learning in the Inner Worlds, it can only be accomplished in the physical dimensions of earth.

Heaven is our Homeland

What should stand out in putting together our perspective of heaven and earth is that heaven is our true homeland; it is where we spend far and away the larger portion of our existence. What determines these glorious intervals when we return to our homeland and how long we stay varies with the individual. There are circumstances when the intervals are brief and circumstances when they are extended, all contingent on our karma. For the vast majority of souls, however, a rule of thumb would be an interval of about 200 years. The older the soul, the less frequent the need to return and, for them, intervals of several hundred years are not uncommon and those of one to two thousand years not unknown.

Circumstances that shorten the gap are dying at an early age, thus leaving little opportunity for progress, and leading a life in which growth and change were notably absent. Circumstances which lengthen the gap are, by contrast, a well-lived life rich in transformation, or one where a more advanced soul is preparing to serve the Hierarchy and needs the additional time to lay the foundation for a number of skills and capacities he or she will manifest in the future incarnation.

The Kindel Archangel

Many years before a soul is due to reincarnate, the meeting with the Kindel Archangel takes place, resulting in the formation of the Incarnation Disc. Some of the items determined at this time are the selection of one's parents and the circumstances under which the individual will begin a new life. With this focus on the upcoming return to earth, the soul now attends events in the Halls of Learning and the Halls of Wisdom, the two great inner schools that possess fascinating resources to enrich one's insight and readiness. It is in these schools that we have access to great souls who illuminate the intricacies of evolutionary unfoldment and the importance of a multitude of opportunities that lie ahead. It is a profoundly promising period during which we glimpse possibilities and commit ourselves to their fulfillment with excellence.

One of the skills we are called upon to refine at this point is the art of visualization — to look into the future and see what ought to be — and to see it so clearly and graphically that when the time comes to realize it in our earthly lives we will act with conviction and inner awareness. Because we are in the Inner Worlds and vividly realize the potential gains that can be made in the upcoming incarnation, we build a sense of resolve regarding them. In the lifetime to come, when each of these opportunities ripens, we will feel this same resolve again, although without the clarity of context visualized originally in the angelic realm. It is more like an inner prompting—a sudden longing or desire to embark on a new endeavor or enterprise. It might be quite strong and compelling or somewhat vague and fleeting, depending upon our state of consciousness and receptivity. If we are open and responsive, during these golden times in our attentive state, we will feel inspired or inwardly led.

This openness is certainly a gift we will wisely cultivate and encourage. On the other hand, should it be wedged in among a host of other conflicting desires or demands that we have allowed into our lives, its signal may become lost in the surrounding hubbub.

Emerging at this juncture is the formation of one of life's most vital forces: that inward calling that summons one to action. It often comes like a voice out of the blue and if it is ignored or resisted, we subsequently feel we have missed an important opportunity. Heeding it, we feel expectant and mantled and that all is right with the world.

Under the best circumstances, leaving the peace, beauty and order of heaven and coming to the often chaotic, dull and plodding conditions of earth is not something to which one looks forward. Two things ease the burden of changing worlds. First, the merciful fact that few of us have more than a vague memory of what the Inner Worlds were like, saves us from a feeling of being imprisoned or banished into exile. Second, is the knowledge that in preparing to make the descent into the material dimension, the earth is the one place where we can make progress and eventually become free of its hold.

The Awakening

There is a third incentive that, when it happens, makes all the difference. This incentive incorporates the art of visualization, receiving inner promptings, and having the sense of a calling in one's life—it is the *awakening*. If we look upon life as a journey that takes us from the lowlands of everyday perception to the highlands of enlightenment, the point separating the two is the moment when we awaken to the reality of God and the Inner Worlds.

What we are dealing with in this illuminating breakthrough is not just our beliefs, but our *experience*. This is what separates our view of life seen through the basic five senses from the transformation that comes with what is called the *sixth sense*. To experience something beyond the immediate range of our physical senses brings us to the gateway of intuition and inner sensing. It can manifest in numerous ways. For some it is a radiance around people or plants, a haunting strain of music, or a mysterious fragrance. Perhaps its most frequent form is an insight, an impression, or a sudden awareness that solves a problem, answers a question, sounds a warning, or illuminates a truth. But what is essential is that, through the sixth sense, Angels gain our attention, instruct, and guide us: an insight emphasized throughout this book.

Beyond our own discomfort in leaving behind the perfection of the heaven worlds, is the quiet, irresistible force of evolution that underlies all of life. It plays out like the enchanting theme of a symphonic masterpiece, wrapping majestically around us, stirring awake our souls, setting our hearts beating to its pulse, assuring us that there is

purpose and destiny to every breath we take, every move we make.

Embracing these commanding impressions, the time comes when we commence our descent. It is then that we meet the resplendent *Angel of Birth*. Of Archangel rank, and always feminine, each one serves hundreds of souls resting and waiting in the mental plane of the Inner Worlds. It is during this time that she assists these souls waiting to be born with developing a certain clarification of consciousness that includes a degree of objective insight and a desire to make good for past mistakes.

When these conditions have been realized, the waiting souls are released into the astral world where they make final preparations for the birth experience.

Angels of Birth are extremely tall and more loving than anyone we have known on earth. In their mantling of earth-destined souls, they bless and counsel them continually, helping them become desirous of the events that lie ahead, or at least accepting of the idea. It is through this Angel's own special powers that, at conception, the life seed of the particular individual whom this woman will raise as her own child, is drawn into the mother's aura. All during the birth experience, the incoming soul is bidding farewell to the colorful, musical world he or she is temporarily leaving behind. The last, wondrous, caring face seen before physical life severs all remembrance, is that of this joyous, compassionate Angel standing at the gateway of birth, sending forth one final sunburst of her radiant, reassuring love.

The incoming soul, enveloped in forgetfulness and surrendered helplessness, crosses the threshold separating the

Inner Worlds from life on earth. It is an experience analogous to descending from a sunlit mountain peak into a fog-shrouded valley at its foot. All of the beauty and wonder of our eternal homeland disappears from view and we are wrapped in what seems a deep sleep. As the period of infancy unfolds, we slowly become conscious of our surroundings and those chosen individuals who make up our family and immediate circle of close contacts. These early years of one's incarnation are carefully programmed for each of us. In the language of the Kindel Angel and in terms of the Incarnation Disc, they are composed of closed keys. Most of us are basically reconstructing our place on the path when last we walked the byways of earth.

As important as childhood is to the formation of our capabilities and characteristics, all of the circumstances that underlie these personal attributes flow out of the wellsprings of our karmic past. We grow up a better person by having good parents who make wise choices for their children and provide them with a loving home and constructive opportunities. It is intellectually tempting to let the matter rest there and credit the parents for our beneficial outcomes when in fact we rightly earned these good parents by our actions in our previous incarnation. This leads to the interesting conclusion that the first decade, and more, of life is largely predetermined by our karma. In this sense, nearly all of the growth that characterizes these rapidly changing years is actually the recapitulation of what was gained in previous lifetimes. The new growth emerging from the present incarnation does not enter the picture until around the onset of adolescence. By this time the basic background of earned attributes has been put in place and new choices with new consequences are beginning to present themselves.

The Watcher Angels

Up until this juncture we come under the attentive care of *Watcher Angels* who are the youngest members of the Angels of Destiny. They are the principal angelic attendants for all children from birth to puberty and continue throughout the adult lives of most of their charges who as yet have not awakened to the experience of God. For those who have awakened to God's reality and whose intuitions are actively receptive to inner promptings, comes a *Guardian Angel*. This marks the beginning of a truly extraordinary relationship—the longest continuing partnership between a human and an Angel in all creation.

It is a liaison that lasts for thousands of years and sees the human through his or her most formative lives of higher unfoldment. But first, we need to understand the role of the Angel known as the Watcher.

Watcher Angels come to their responsibilities after having served as helpers under the Angels of Birth and Death in the region of the Akashic Records. They also have assisted both the Angels of Healing and those of Prayer, two ranks of Angels discussed in the following chapter. Thus, their background has brought them close to humanity's most vital gateways and quests for divine intervention. There are both male and female Watcher Angels each of whom is responsible for at least seven individuals. To the extent allowed by the karmic histories of each person under their care, they provide protection, guidance, and the mantling of light.

With all that goes wrong in the lives of both children and adults, a common question is why are not the efforts of these beings more effective? First of all, we might best discover how effective they indeed are if God suddenly withdrew them from service altogether. We would then realize how much worse things could be without them. More to the point, Angels are not among us to spare us the consequences of our mistakes or shortcomings or to make the way smooth and painless. They are present to support the aim of human destiny: to learn and to grow in consciousness and character and, ultimately, to become self-emptied and God-filled.

Watchers, as do all Angels, possess the attributes of selfless love and a consuming interest in the perfecting of life. Given the condition of the vast numbers of people on the earth today and their preoccupation with survival and self-interest, Watchers also must be profoundly patient and visionary to endure the slow pace of our progress.

It is of course the great good fortune of humanity that Watchers and all other Angels possess these qualities and more.

Watchers are permitted to choose certain spheres, localities, and countries in which to serve. Often they grow so fond of a particular vicinity that they will remain active there for thousands of human years. Others will move through the atmosphere of earth invisibly serving the needs of persons wherever they are led to help.

There are other noteworthy features of these faithful servers. Take the example of a Watcher who happens to be male and who has a particular man among his responsibilities. The Watcher began attending that individual from the moment of his physical birth. It is possible that the Watcher would take responsibility, not only for the one man, but for all the members of this man's immediate family in his encirclement. When this man leaves the physical world, he leaves the territory supervised by this Watcher angel. Unless this individual incarnates again into the same country, and particularly into the identical vicinity, he is unlikely to again meet the Watcher who earlier looked after him. But in his following lifetime, the human, wherever he is born, will once more be taken into the loving and helpful consideration of one of these steadfast beings.

Watchers are inclined to develop a fondness for a particular one of their numerous charges. Thus, the time arrives in later stages of advancement wherein the Watcher exercises a potent influence over the destiny of a given individual. It follows from this evolutionary unfoldment that thousands of years before a mortal is ready and worthy of the steadfast assistance of a Guardian Angel, a Watcher, who is destined to join the ranks of Guardians, chooses her charge.

This last observation calls attention to a significant difference between the two Angel ranks.

The Guardian Angels

Whereas Watchers are either male or female, the Guardian Angel is always feminine, for she is our spiritual mother coming to us when the spiritual side of our nature begins to stir. Thus, it is that the feminine Watchers advance to the Guardian rank. The masculine Watchers, in their turn, advance to a rank known as the Protectors. Eventually they join the legions of Warrior Angels serving the Archangel Michael whose mission is the scattering of darkness and the triumph of the Light.

Guardian Angels await the moment when a person has realized awakenment—that transcendent breakthrough when our entire being is invaded by an outpouring of Divinity that transforms consciousness. It is then that we no longer simply believe in God—we *know* Him through our own personal, immediate experience. When that threshold has been crossed, the gates of inner perception at last are beginning to open, and we set out on the great and final journey of human evolution: illumination and initiation. It will take us across many lifetimes and through a fascinating sequence of adventures. In making the journey, we will be called upon to conquer our egos and all of their attachments. At the same time we will make contact with our souls and higher consciousness and undertake the transformation of character that signifies our evolutionary progress.

Flower has described the appearance of the Guardian Angel. As for her features, it is her face that stands out, nearly obscuring all the rest of her in detail and brightness. Her eyes are large and express a fathomless depth of love.

Her aura is predominantly pale pink with degrees of shading that vary with each individual charge. The tones of pink are vibrant, often resembling a pulsating heart. The heart center itself radiates a golden hue and the whole aura at times can appear as rose. She stands at the right side of her charge and is beautiful beyond imagination. Accompanying her outshining presence are the sparkling thought forms of highest impulses, new disciplines, resolves, and insights she patiently and lovingly broadcasts.

Guardian Angels express their happiness by smiling, but not in simply a pleased or amused manner. Their smile comes from the Soul and sends forth a burst of color. Its radiation is a mingling of burnished gold and peach, if one can imagine such a blend. It shines out from their auras and if you are touched by it you share a moment of great upliftment. Their happiness is apt to be most outflowing when their human charge rises above a long-standing temptation or entrenched negative habit.

Her work, tirelessly and with undiminished enthusiasm, is to awaken, inspire, and guide her charge throughout the hours of each day. Considering the conflicting preoccupations of the human ego, her steadfastness is monumental. She is ever the teacher, pointing out shortcomings that need correction or promising opportunities that offer growth. Her thoroughgoing manner leaves no stone unturned that might strengthen our character or refine our awareness. If we make a mistake, her uncompromising honesty, always bathed in love, underscores what went wrong and why. By whatever means it takes to grasp our attention, she makes certain we get the message. The still greater challenge is to prod us into doing what must be done to resolve the need or problem.

Her communication with us can take a number of forms. Only when one has an exceptional degree of clairvoyance, such as Flower possessed, can the Guardian directly instruct her charge. There was, of course, an added advantage to those close to such a channel. It was not uncommon for Flower to relay instruction from the Guardians among her students by saying to one of them, "Your Guardian tells me it is important for you to bring a pet into your home." Or to other students she might relay that their Guardian felt it was time for them to take a course in public speaking or to see a specialist about their health. As she explained, Flower did not hear a voice in these contacts. Angels send forth thought forms that become words as they enter her consciousness.

At night, our Guardian Angel initiates us into the mysteries of life. She accompanies us on nightly excursions into specially selected dimensions of the Inner Worlds. It might be a visit to the Halls of Learning or Halls of Wisdom in Shamballa, the center where the earth's inner government resides; or perhaps to witness a gathering of Great Souls in the New Jerusalem honoring our Lord Christ. Whatever the destination, our Guardian chooses one that is timely, instructive and illuminating. It is also she who, during dreams of psychological significance, becomes our mentor and revealer.

Flower's Guardian on three memorable occasions saved her from serious harm and possibly saved her life. When she was still a child, she was riding with her mother and a married couple through a mountainous region of Pennsylvania. A dense blanket of fog lay across the land and the driver was fighting off drowsiness. Suddenly, Flower's Guardian sent her a flashing signal that they were in grave danger. Flower cried out a warning to the driver to immediately stop the car.

No sooner was this done than a speeding train whizzed past their car now halted before a poorly marked railroad crossing.

Then there was an incident when Flower was still in her teens and was walking through Exposition Park in Los Angeles with an adult friend, Mrs. Smith. Their destination was a nearby armory where Mrs. Smith's husband was in charge of drilling men for the military service. It was in the twilight period and growing rather dark, when suddenly they became aware that they were being followed. The faster they walked, the faster advanced the two men following them. At that point Flower prayed to her Guardian for protection. Suddenly, out from the shrubbery came a large St. Bernard dog. Strangely, it closely resembled one Flower had as a companion when she was three years old. The dog turned and faced the approaching men. One of them was heard to whisper, "Oh, they have a dog with them." The St. Bernard then accompanied Flower and her friend all the way to the steps of the armory. In gratitude, Flower turned to touch the dog, but it had vanished as mysteriously as it had appeared. She was certain that her Guardian had been instrumental in superphysically manifesting the image of her childhood pet.

On another occasion she and her husband Lawrence were driving along a busy highway in the winter. As they started down a steep hillside, they encountered sheets of ice which caused them to lose control of the car and hurtle toward a crowded intersection at the bottom of the hill. To her amazement, she saw their car enveloped in what appeared to be a huge block of ice which gently eased them into a soft snow bank. Onlookers quickly gathered around them, sharing their remarkable deliverance from what would have been a tragic collision.

Even more remarkable, Flower's Guardian has been instrumental in her overcoming a long-standing fear. She shared how she overcame a dread of water, going back to a former incarnation in Yucatan when as a young woman she was thrown into a cenote, a huge natural well, as a sacrifice to appease the rain god. Because she died struggling, she was left with this terror of drowning.

One night when she was 14 years old, her Guardian, realizing the time had come for Flower to conquer this fear, waited until she was asleep, then took her in her astral body to an inner shrine. There before her unbelieving eyes lay the same well of sacrifice where, ten incarnations earlier, she had lost her life. Repulsed, she drew back but her Guardian gestured in a manner that Flower knew she had to obey if ever this fear was to be mastered. She let herself fall into the great well, strangely forgetting that this was on the Inner Planes and she was in no real physical danger — a phenomenon common to an individual undergoing such a test. As she went down and down in that pool, a lion suddenly appeared ahead of her and she caught hold of his mane. Instantly, it lunged, pulling her into a temple-like underwater grotto. The lion gave a shake and, to her amazement, there in its place stood her Guardian, smiling triumphantly. Flower's fear of water had entirely vanished.

Even before this instance, experiences with her Guardian were a regular part of her growing up. This began in earnest when she was ten. At this early time of her youth she was instructed to begin attending the Sunday school of a church which was soon to sponsor a Girl Scout troop. In the years that followed, she was counseled by this glorious presence to attend certain concerts and cultural events, to visit libraries and museums.

She would even take her small lunch allowance and go to the finer restaurants in her community, ordering perhaps only a bowl of soup, in the interest of acquiring self-reliance and some of the social graces afforded by such establishments.

Flower's first lesson in the superficiality of glamour came when she was six years old. She went with her mother to visit a relative in a hospital. The ward where this person was kept was a large open room containing at least twelve beds. What immediately caught her attention was a woman who must have been the head nurse, going from bed to bed, as were several other nurses. Flower was fascinated by the light that radiated from this selfless individual; it lit up the entire ward. To Flower, the auras of each of the other nurses appeared bright as well. Flower was caught up in what appeared to be the spirituality of this profession, an impression that she assumed made every nurse virtuous.

Her Guardian made no comment, but on a subsequent visit to the same ward a few days later, the head nurse was not present and the other nurses were going about their duties uninspiredly. Flower, looking around, was surprised to see how pale the auras of these same nurses had become. This left her puzzled and somewhat disenchanted with that profession for several years. When she was ten, her Guardian reminded her of this incident and how it had reduced her hero worship toward nurses. Then her Guardian observed, "Do not imagine that all persons of authority are virtuous or have strong characters. Look at what their auras indicate when they are under pressure or lack inspired leadership, and you will know whether or not they are exemplary." From that time forward, Flower did not take anyone as an authority figure unless such a person's inner brightness was sufficiently steadfast to merit recognition.

This caution also held true for individuals who were outwardly very attractive, having earned in the past the right to a handsome or beautiful body. More times than not, such persons failed to possess a corresponding inner beauty.

In the absence of someone with Flower's gift, it is far more common, especially if it involves a needed correction, for the Angel to make use of someone who is in a position to bring the fault to our attention. While we might not readily associate this as coming from our Guardian, we are made aware of what she sees standing in the way of our progress and a foundation is in place for her to build upon.

For instance, when someone calls attention to a fault they see in us, the human reaction too often is to discount criticism by "considering the source." We rationalize that so and so is envious or prejudiced and pay no heed to the fault expressed. A far wiser course of action would be to set our defense mechanisms aside—our denials—and consider to what extent the criticism could be valid and go to work on that.

Another familiar occurrence is pangs of conscience. While we attribute these to origins in dealing with our parents and society, the truth is the Guardian has often had a hand in forging our conscience behind the scenes. While not all aspects of conscience are wholesome and constructive — especially an overburden of guilt — we soon recognize those proddings that bring us out into the light inviting our pursuit. Then there are promptings and inner impressions which typically come to us out of nowhere and point us in the direction of putting long neglected things right or making a fresh start on overlooked endeavors. These experiences are to be particularly sought after as they invite our conscious preparation and perception.

Yet another medium through which the Guardian frequently engages our attention is through dreams. In particular, dreams often underscore what we are neglecting. If we master the language of dreams, which is usually in the guise of the most vivid and plainspoken symbolism, it unerringly guides us to a frank dramatization of our neglect.

Take, for example, the common occurrence of a dream in which we are due to give a lecture or appear before an important audience, only to suddenly realize we are unkempt and dressed in ragged, dirty clothing. Plainly, the dream is pointing out that we are not well prepared in life and we need to make this a priority. Another theme that dreams reflect is that of compensation. If our waking personalities are one sided, such that we are preoccupied with the practical side of life and are prone to be critical of people who are more creative and visionary, the dream casts us in the role of one who is altogether impractical.

One last strategy our Guardian uses to call our shortcomings into account, and perhaps the most effective, is the nature of our circumstances. As we encounter those conditions in life that we have attracted karmically, we inevitably come face to face with our next steps of growth. She expectantly awaits these encounters since they are the rich and fertile grounds whereby we eventually harvest our overcomings and our transformations. The Guardian does not focus on spectacular breakthroughs but upon the little steps of progress that, daily, lift us a bit farther along the path as we journey Godward. If we are prone to be neglectful, it is the little things that first get ignored. Knowing this, she works painstakingly with us to "be masterly in little things."

The Guardian Angel, as a sort of spiritual mother loves her charge with an emotion a thousand times stronger than what a human mother is capable of, such is the purity and refinement of her feeling nature. She is beyond the vicissitudes of emotion with which humans struggle. Still, she is not one to mince words, or spare us the truth. In this respect, she is our greatest critic, never missing an opportunity to smooth our rough edges.

Although she holds none of our weaknesses against us, there are three qualities she will not tolerate. The first is insincerity which compromises our integrity. Second is taking things for granted which signals the absence of gratitude. And third is facetiousness which belittles truth and goodness.

As our spiritual mother and teacher, she is constantly finding ways to elicit our higher nature. Since no negative states ever enter her consciousness, she patiently shepherds us toward that eventual conquest in ourselves. In the meantime, her merriment and joy comes when we successfully meet a test or surmount a challenge. She wisely knows that when our lives are summarized, the only moments that merit recognition are those that advance our evolution. Understandably, our progress, therefore, represents a gauge of our Guardian's progress as our teacher. To this end, she often confronts us with testing circumstances so that we will become aware of our needs and unfinished business. If any of these encounters have us battling darkness beyond our ability to cope, she will be there fighting harder for us than we could possibly do ourselves, for she is indeed our Guardian.

Angels very seldom praise us, preferring to avoid the reinforcement praise provides the ego. The Guardian's single aim is her charge's progress Godward and every occasion that lends itself to that end is one for rejoicing.

In her role as teacher, the Guardian often finds it necessary to call faults and shortcomings to our attention. She does this in whatever manner is available to her at the moment — through an awakening realization, the comments of others, or a chain of insightful circumstances. Her motive is to get us moving to correct the deficiency. Her criticism is like spiritual surgery, for it removes the offending trait and opens the door to healing and transformation.

Guardian Angels commune with us in various ways. They have the most direct access to our soul or higher self. Impressions that come to us from this source are like insights or inspired realizations that suddenly appear in our consciousness, unforeseen and fully formed. The Guardian will often call to our attention certain circumstances or events which are important to our spiritual wellbeing—perhaps a vital meeting or an opportunity. Some individuals are even sensitive to particular fragrances such as lilies of the valley or roses, that announce the presence of their Guardians. Others are reminded of their Guardians by certain signs or symbols that appear unexpectedly.

A noteworthy attribute of a Guardian Angel is her change of position when she has something important to communicate. Although she ordinarily appears to the right of her charge, at significant times she places herself squarely in front of the one she is about to instruct. This occurred to Flower when she was 15 years old, sitting on the back porch of their home in Scranton, Pennsylvania. All at once, she saw her Guardian fully in front of her. Flower knew something unusual was about to be announced. The date was September 18,

1924, and her Guardian informed her that she and her family were to be in California by November 18th.

It might as well have been Timbuktu for they had never entertained the notion of leaving Pennsylvania or the East Coast. Although Flower's mother had her own human limitations, she nevertheless had faith in her daughter's clairvoyance and two months later they found themselves in Los Angeles. This locale became the springboard for Flower's future work.

The behavior of a Guardian can be delightfully subtle and mysterious. Flower fondly remembers an incident that took place near the end of World War II. She had been lecturing in Palm Springs and was returning home to Questhaven Retreat near Escondido with her husband, Lawrence. As they followed along the Palms to Pines Highway, passing through the San Jacinto mountains, Lawrence noted a turnoff to a place called Idyllwild. Feeling drawn to explore this unfamiliar mountain village, he turned to Flower and proposed having a look. She was tired from the lecture engagement and aware of the multiplicity of duties awaiting their return, but seeing the brightness of Lawrence's aura she realized his interest was prompted by his own Guardian. So they drove the few miles up to this quaint alpine community.

As soon as they rounded the last turn that revealed its magnificent setting, Flower caught her breath in surprise. Here was her heart's desire for a mountain hideaway. Nestled in a bowl-shaped valley a mile high, surrounded on three sides by inspiring peaks, and containing a splendid forest of fir, pine, and cedar, Idyllwild was a gift from heaven.

It was then that she noticed her own Guardian who was smiling with a sunburst of light as only an Angel can. Hav-

64

ing foreseen what lay in store for her charge, the Guardian chose to be unobtrusive, remaining in the background, awaiting the inevitable moment of discovery.

Idyllwild was to become Flower's home away from home—her place of personal retreat and renewal, thanks to the resourcefulness of her husband's Guardian.

It was a place she and her Guardian spent some of their happiest and most fulfilling times. One period in particular stood out for Flower. She was preparing a series of lessons for an upcoming weeklong retreat. As Questhaven was the focal point of so many needs and duties, she went to her mountain home for freedom and uplift. Still the weight of deadlines burdened her. In the morning she took up her journal and said to herself, "I've had enough! I do not need to live with a consciousness oppressed by too many things to do. I can be free!" She then set out to walk on a mountain trail. But even her ardent prayers and the freshness of the scene were not enough to ease her mind.

She came at last to a tree that she loved. Leaning against it, she looked up and breathed one deeper prayer. "There must be freedom, release, and peace. Teach me!" At that moment her Guardian spoke to her, "Look up and be impressed by what you see." Obeying this request, Flower looked up into the beautiful azure sky with scattered puffs of white clouds moving across the blue expanse in freedom, order and ecstatic serenity. There was no hurry. There was no pressure. There was only a purifying immensity. It rinsed her free of the day's burden, restoring her peace and freedom.

She did not know how long she stood watching the vaulted heavens, but suddenly her mind began to receive instruction from her soul about the empowerment of the immensity of consciousness itself. Like opening a floodgate, the themes of the lessons she needed to prepare poured out on the pages of her journal.

For Flower, it was a life-changing experience. The Guardian is especially gifted in helping us find lost articles or misplaced documents. Faced with such circumstances Flower would pause, bringing herself to centeredness in God, and reverently invoke the attention of her Guardian to the need at hand. Invariably, the missing item would soon turn up. In the same manner, if she herself ever became lost in a forest wilderness or foreign city, she would once again call upon her Guardian to find her way back to her point of origin.

Human souls which have the honor of mantling by a Guardian Angel, are wise to remember that she has selected her charge from among all the human candidates she has observed over thousands of earth years when she was a Watcher Angel. Her choice was based on seeing the possibilities of this individual, alongside the many immaturities and even glaring shortcomings that yet exist.

Your Guardian loves you more than anyone you have ever known in the outer dimension. She is indeed your spiritual mother and she will support and help you as no one else in human form ever can. She is your greatest comfort and will never fail you. As your spiritual teacher, she will do everything in her power to direct you toward higher unfoldment. Above all else, she will do whatever she can to keep you on course steadily climbing the Mountain of God. Her great joy is for you to recognize and seek out her guidance and instruction. The Guardian's natural grasp of what is possible will always assign much more for you to accomplish than you feel capable of delivering. She brightly expects you to grow faster and reach farther than you thought possible. This is not to see you fail, but to see you extend well beyond your perceived limitations, surprising you with hidden potentials.

Still, there are times when the Guardian will choose not to be so full of instruction. As our own capabilities mature, she will simply observe us for a period of time to see how well we have mastered our lessons. However, when a need arises and we face a challenge in our relationships or a crisis in health, she will come once again to the foreground and impress upon our conscious minds what steps need to be taken.

The destiny of a Guardian Angel is to enter the ranks of the Great Archangels. Already advanced, she will be permitted to become either an Angel of Birth or Angel of Transition, or if she chooses, to join the ranks of still other Archangel Orders serving humanity.

Next to God, the Lord Christ, and the Holy Spirit, our Guardian is our greatest benefactor; our debt to her can only be repaid through steadfastly striving Godward.

Angels Serving
the Christ

70

A great company of Angels exists whose sole purpose is to serve the Lord Christ. Altogether, they span the region of the Inner Worlds that attends to worship, healing, prayer, and initiation. Collectively, they are thought of as "religious" Angels, since they are most often observed clairvoyantly around churches, temples, and sacred spaces. Their work is to bring individuals closer to God consciousness. Against the background of worldly thought and preoccupations, these resplendent beings plant the seeds of worship and wonder that undergird religious faith and set the stage for the experience of the mystical. They also are messengers of healing and wholeness, encompassing physical, emotional, and mental needs.

It is important to point out that the Lord Christ embraces all religions and all aspirants Godward. In His own words, "In my Father's House are many mansions." The multitude of earthly divisions among all the branches of the tree of life ascending to mastery are reflections of human creativeness, on the one hand, and oftentimes human pride and ambition, on the other. One would be hard pressed to document the multiplicity of pathways to God, let alone their tributaries, that humanity has fashioned throughout the ages. What counts in each of these expressions of worship is the presence of an ascending consciousness accompanied with the fulfillment of a code of conduct worthy of a disciple living the life and following the way. We have traveled too many paths across too many lifetimes for it to be otherwise.

Angels of Adoration

The most numerous of the company of Angels serving the Lord Christ are known as *Angels of Adoration*. They especially attend churches, religious shrines, and all places where worship and reverence are *sincerely* practiced.

They send forth waves of radiant rose-colored energy, mingling with auric tones of blue, yellow, and green. They are alert to the slightest sign of a genuine spiritual need within a congregation. Their principal endeavor is to lift the consciousness of those in attendance by purifying and encouraging every individual who is open to Divine Presence.

They are, by nature, the most joyous beings Flower has ever observed. Entire audiences are enveloped in the auras of these tireless workers. To behold the resulting transformation of the congregation is fascinating, for the whole gathering is suffused in an atmosphere of changing colors which gradually become brighter and purer. The speaker especially is mantled by this angelic outpouring of joy and surcharging of power. Seen from this viewpoint, a religious service could never again be experienced in a perfunctory manner. It is indeed a celebration of these wondrous beings such that not to respond in kind would be closed-minded and cold-hearted.

Even when a cathedral or chapel is empty, several Angels of Adoration remain in attendance to keep active the reverent energies of the place of worship. During a service, the number of these dedicated servers will increase many fold, depending on the number and needs of the congregation. They go about their delightful duties with such enthusiasm that the reservoir of renewal and consecration they generate flows out into the surrounding community, touching even disinterested passersby who nevertheless receive a baptism of peace as they go on their way.

During the service, the Angels of Adoration strive to awaken passive individuals, prompting them to see the light that active engagement of spiritual principles makes possible.

If there are those among the congregation who are discouraged, they are helped to be relieved of their self-preoccupation. Those seeking truth are sensitized to key statements of the speaker, perhaps also through exchanges with fellow worshipers following the service. In all instances, if people were to become aware of the luminous presences about them, they would witness beauty impossible to describe. They would behold the most magnificent faces looking down upon them from billowing cloud-like thresholds of opal and coral tones. This overseeing refines the consciousness of those present, helping them expand their receptivity to transforming energies.

In every gathering of worshipers, much darkness is present. This is because humans characteristically accumulate mental and emotional burdens as each week unfolds. It is the work of these radiant Angels of Adoration, even before the service begins, to systematically separate these dark residues from the more fragrant, colorful, and reverent thought forms and feelings spontaneously arising from the innermost aspirations of each member of the congregation. Once separated, these positive emanations then move heavenward.

Half of the Angels of Adoration stand at full attention, separating and willing the sediment of human thoughts to disappear far below the chapel's foundation into the body of the Planetary Logos' white fiery Spirit. The other half consecrate themselves to lifting Godward the sincere yet immature and imperfect spiritual strivings rising from the congregation, all the while blending them with their own luminous essences.

As the worshiper develops rapport through deep sincerity, and is filled with thanksgiving for the Highest, it is at last possible for these shining ones to act directly upon an individual's consciousness.

All the while, they increase the tempo of devotion and expand the aura of the place of worship. The means of achieving this involves angelic invocations which are answered by invisible presences responding to their calls in a most heartwarming manner.

The highest service given by the Angels of Adoration is to take what seed thoughts they gather from humans and relay them into the higher keeping of other orders of Angels above them. These, in turn, will carry out a successive relaying ministry until these devotions become a part of the fragrant incense of holiness which the lofty *Seraphim* gather and offer unceasingly to the One who is Holiest.

During religious services when a group has gathered for reverent worship, Angels of Adoration are constantly in motion. Seen clairvoyantly, thought waves from individuals go forth, including waves created by hymns, prayers, meditations, and rituals. The Angels dip into these waves, mold them into useful patterns, and focus strong spiritual radiations upon persons in need of special assistance. Every sincere group that mentions God is like a signal fire, attracting Angels who serve to strengthen the bond of communion between God and aspiring human channels. And, once again, the quality they exude most strongly and distinctly, in Flower's experience, is a fervent joy.

Angels of Song

Assisting the Angels of Adoration to lift the human spirit are *Angels of Song*. They are the source of the legendary Music of the Spheres. Many, if not all, of the great composers, knowingly or unknowingly, have been inspired by these song-uttering Angels whose creations stir the souls of all who are sensitive to the strains of their unending melodies. Wagner, in particular, was receptive to this source. The singing of these Angels can be likened to humming, for they express tones, never words.

In a talk given during a Michaelmas Retreat, Flower described the means by which these Angels generate their incomparable tones. It involves what, on first glance, resembles a trumpet, but in fact is a tube-like energy field around which currents move. The Angels then create tones that enter this hollow energy formation. These tones are purified and amplified by angelic vibrations until they come forth with a power and glory unknown to the human. They contain such a sense of joy and clarity of sound as they flow into the ethers that the very heavens reverberate with their peace-giving upliftment.

When channeled and self-emptied singers tune into these frequencies, their voices will echo the call tones of these Angels with an unbelievable quality and range. It is the same when the members of a choir sing with selfless devotion, tapping into these sources. The audience feels tingling sensations throughout their physical bodies and the glory of the music resounds in mind and spirit for a long, long time.

Needless to say, Flower cherished music as a means of lifting the human spirit and creating the atmosphere of worship. Every Sunday service she performed and every major three day retreat at Questhaven featured soul-stirring musical performances. It was not unusual for her, at the end of a service, to leave the speaker's podium and join the choir in singing a benediction. What was most moving of all, however, were the occasions when she would sing an Angel call herself, leaving the audience hushed and deeply touched.

Angels of Prayer

In response to the invocations of the Angels of Adoration come the stately, pure, and wise *Angels of Prayer*. They, along with the *Angels of Healing* whom they supervise, are unceasingly attentive to the upreaching of our requests and longings offered in prayer. It is the work of both orders to receive these offerings and to lift them up to the appropriate source in the Inner Worlds.

The Angels of Prayer are another grade higher than the Angels of Adoration from whose ranks they have risen. Their purpose is to study the consciousness of groups and their individual members. Their splendid, lofty height and their penetrating, understanding presence provides releasement to the many troubled hearts they have silently counseled. It is their wish to leave within the aura of every individual who is receptive, a vision, an impetus, or a realization as to his or her further progress and improvement.

Angels of Prayer have white auras and are usually robed in dazzling light so that their faces stand out as their most distinguishable feature. Their temperament is noticeably reserved, and always regal in bearing. They watch, strengthen, and assist in the transitions our prayers and meditations undergo as they are received and answered. They safefold our constructive thoughts so that they will progress to a higher source free from interference. Unworthy thoughts or appeals never reach their level.

To one with clairvoyance, our prayers are like seeds which have seasons of blossoming and fruitfulness. The love these bright messengers send forth to protect and nourish our uplifted inspirations is a gift for which we can ever be grateful. Flower recalls observing one such Angel's efforts regarding an individual's prayer for the wellbeing of loved ones during a long absence.

As the pink, winged thought form moved from the person praying toward the home where the loved one resided, a stately Angel of Prayer intercepted the homing thought form. After several moments it appeared as though a searchlight of purest white essence shone directly above the mental image. Slowly the image began to expand, all the while increasing in size and changing color from a glowing pink to a pinkish-white form undulating with a breathing motion. Tracing the prayer form to its destination, Flower saw it tended and watched over by the beloved Angel of the Place, guardian of the home. This glorious presence then added her own flame of encirclement about the human prayer, enhancing the breathing motion and causing it to emit an exquisite fragrance.

Angels of Healing

Working closely with the Angels of Prayer and under their supervision are the Angels of Healing. Their auras are a medium blue and they respond to definite appeals for assistance. This brings them swiftly to the side of the sick or injured. Flower has watched these servers gently comb the auras of patients to rid them of harmful accumulations of negativity. When the physical and astral bodies are stirred by such cleansing, the life force enters harmoniously once again and the afflicted return to health and wellbeing. In addition to working with patients, Healing Angels inspire doctors and nurses, telepathically advising the right treatment for each case. However, if for karmic reasons the life cycle of the patient has come to its rightful conclusion, whether that be in childhood or maturity, the Healing Angels do not interfere with the law governing transition.

These Healing Angels with their blue auras are most wonderful to watch.

Flower has seen them in hospitals where pain auras were so dark that it was difficult for one with inner sight to enter such a heavy atmosphere. Yet these Healing Angels would be there combing the hospital's aura, ridding it of the congestion and lifting the smog of suffering, especially from the rooms of greatest need. They work for depression to be replaced by hope; for pain to give way to peace.

The work of healing is not the exclusive province of Healing Angels. They are often joined by Angels of Prayer. Flower, for example, describes an occasion when a close associate had to undergo serious surgery. Knowing that this involved a prolonged operation, Flower prayed that the Lord Christ would send His emissaries. Once the surgery was underway, Flower tuned in to the operating room and saw a lavender mist flooding the entire area. When the shade of lavender reached a certain clarity and purity, at the head of the patient appeared two stalwart Angels of Prayer. The one standing at the right of his head concentrated on the chief surgeon. The other Angel standing on the left was completely absorbed in sustaining the patient's physical and etheric bodies, since the higher bodies had been detached. This Angel channeled a constant flow of light, soft yellow in essence, that moved from the patient's head down through his feet. It left his body somewhat darker in color because it was rinsing out the sediment of the illness that had accumulated in the etheric region, much like the color of laundry water when rinsing out work clothes. It was an insight that deepened her appreciation of these tireless and noble beings.

Flower has observed that there are always a number of Healing Angels about a hospital. As prayers of individual patients and their anxious friends and relatives rise up, their number increases proportionately.

They first determine whether or not the patient is due to undergo transition or, instead, to begin the healing process. If the investigation reveals that the person's life span is not yet finished, they first focus on arresting the progress of the illness or afflicted condition, then make a concerted effort to enlighten the consciousness of the patient. They next go to work to prompt doctors to arrive at accurate diagnoses and beneficial treatment.

Whether a medical specialist prescribes or a metaphysician prays, help from the higher dimensions attends those in need. In the coming Aquarian Age, Flower tells us, we will be able to telepathically communicate directly with Healing Angels. Then these clear-seeing presences can inform us of even the most obscure causes of our debilities and instruct us step by step in the healing process that re-

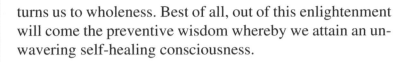

turns us to wholeness. Best of all, out of this enlightenment will come the preventive wisdom whereby we attain an unwavering self-healing consciousness.

Angels of the Christ Presence

Above the Angels of Prayer and Angels of Healing are the magnificent *Angels of the Christ Presence* — these are at the stage of Archangel evolution. This triumphant spirit of light is always masculine. The more one thinks of, aspires toward, and invokes the presence and spirit of the Lord Christ, the stronger and more available becomes one's link with an Angel of this rank and relationship to our Lord. Each one of these exalted beings is an emissary of the Christ and shares in the fulfillment of His mission. When any group meets sincerely in recognition of His Reality, an Angel of the Christ Presence will be there.

This unique order of angelic beings exists perpetually within the Lord Emmanuel's realm of service to undergird His mission and relay His currents of awakening and transformation.

Because of working with the Christ, and of having been trained in the schools and powers of solar baptisms, the Angel of the Christ Presence stands robed and invested in the full qualities of the Christ, which he is reflecting, and of the spiritual Sun radiations with which he is natively endowed.

From the glorious and all-perfect vibrant being who is the Lord Christ, and from the aureole of tremendous spiritual energy around Him, come these mobile representatives whose inner soul beauty shines resplendently like that of the Lord they worship and serve. Angels of the Christ Presence are eternally watchful, for they are most eager to discover new outposts, or altars, from which their resources can be distributed.

The Lord Christ not only radiates energy through such perfected channels, but sends forth the archetypal qualities of divine love, divine purity and divine unselfishness through them as well. Every Master, every Lord, and every Logos adds to the extension of that auric emanation known as the wondrous Christ Spirit. Moreover, all consecrated acts in the world stemming from humans, Angels, or Logoi, add to the vitality of this Christ Light's radiance.

Consider one such Angel of the Christ Presence who abides at Questhaven Retreat in the vicinity of the Church of the Holy Quest. This majestic being is known as the Archangel Mentiel and he is within reach of all worshipers' thoughts wherever they pray. His presence can be felt and known in all the services taking place on the retreat grounds. Meetings, other than those on the Sabbath, might not attract him if the participants were preoccupied with worldly or personal matters and oblivious to the consciousness of worship he ordains. Nevertheless, whenever this great presence is invited, he will respond.

We also meet this Archangel at those times when we overcome a serious habit or an erroneous concept to which we have long clung. In the ecstasy of the Jubilus — that transcendent moment of illumination — he is present as the Initiatory Angel.

These great Angels are found wherever there is *utter sincerity*, for this quality is more vital than the stage of advancement or level of understanding a group has reached in consciousness. Not all churches possess these participants at their altars. If the spirit is dead in these churches, or if the attitudes have crystallized, their altar fires will have grown dim. Not until that time arrives when they are again taught by one whose fiery soul can reawaken the embers of vital, reverent worship will their altar again receive its angelic ensoulment. An Angel of the Christ Presence labors with humanity's soulic fires, and during all consecrated services he endeavors to activate the seeds of God-like qualities that become alive momentarily at the mention of certain realities. An Angel of the Christ Presence works to speak to your spirituality directly, and he endeavors to purify the consciousness of whatever has sullied it in the interim since your last God-contact at a holy place.

During a gathering lasting about an hour, three distinct cleansings will be administered by means of his presence. Through the charging of his commands, purifications will be forced upon the dross which collects around people's lower faculties. First, a baptism of white protective Light is released. This is followed by a second baptism which frees the group, while the service is in session, from the collective powers of testing that accompany any body of people by virtue of being human. The third baptism, which usually comes near the end of an address, energizes the radiation and distribution of the true Christ Spirit among the group. Following these necessary preliminary purifications, a golden light of benediction, which can only come from one who is perfected, is summoned, invoked, and released into the spiritual envelope of the group's consciousness.

These supremely pure ones endeavor, during a gathering on the Sabbath or whenever a congregation is present, to affect the consciousness of each spokesman who might address the group. When the flow of influence is felt or even unknowingly transmitted by the recipient, then an Angel such as the Archangel Mentiel will broadcast his waves of power to the farthest ends of the group, quickening, improving, and deepening the selfless work of the Angels of Adoration. He will cause a tide of force to flow back toward him through the congregation, once again bringing into his aura the full draft of mental impressions, as well as emotional needs or moods that the group is experiencing. In his willing these tides, the ebb and flow of which carry and return his light, he puts to work the important servers: human beings in each group who are known by the term of "pillars." They help to ground his voltage, as it were, and cause these tides to flow more slowly and effectively than they might otherwise.

This transcendent Archangel will lift the entire thought form that has arisen from the group during the worship service. This usually occurs during the final prayer on the Sabbath. What now has become a very large, gloriously colorful, and greatly expanded thought form contains all the prayers and needs of the entire congregation. This Angel of the Christ Presence, through his understanding and power, lifts up the resulting sphere or globe-like emanation into the keeping of the Seraphim.

The Seraphim

It is important to be aware of the fact that the Seraphim in no sense resemble the child-like figures so often idealized by artists and portrayed in their drawings and paintings. The

Seraphim are exceedingly tall, valiant, strong, and mighty creatures of God. Were one of their company to enter the atmosphere of any of the Earth's dedicated sanctuaries, the inner dimensions of such sanctified places would be accompanied by tumultuous, resounding waves of power sufficient to break up the frozen and crystallized attitudes that we humans so typically gravitate toward.

The Seraphim receive unto themselves even the seed thoughts and adorations of the youngest in angelic evolution. In this manner, the thought emanation from the group is wondrously expanded and lifted into the profound and mysterious depths of light beyond the thoughts of humankind and the Angels themselves.

We will be wise to think on these things. Although we might seldom address the Angel of the Christ Presence directly in asking his special help, we would do well in our prayers to remember him who stands before the Presence of the Infinite God, that he may be blessed and enriched through his contact with us whom he quickens so selflessly.

The one we know to be the Lord Christ is Lord of Angels and of men. We realize He is not a single Presence serving alone but heads an immense company of Angels who carry out the details of His office. When we sincerely and reverently pronounce His name in prayer, it summons any number of these angelic hosts. Because they are so in tune with His spirit, we often feel our Lord's presence through their reflection of His distinctive emanation. Thus it is that when we envision the Holy Trinity, it is not simply three transcendent Beings we call upon, but company upon company of Angels joyously, wholeheartedly serving these three fountainheads of Divinity. Beheld in this way, the Kingdom of

God of which our Lord spoke is vast indeed, fully capable of responding to every need.

Angels of
the Holy Spirit

The Third Aspect of Divinity comprises that great company of Angels who serve the Spirit of Truth. They support the venerated *Lord Maha Chohan*, the exalted Being who holds this office, by doing all in their power to bring forth new channels of His wisdom, as well as imparting enlightenment to the individuals they assist.

Awakeners

First and most numerous among the Angels who serve in this way are the *Awakeners*, also known as the *Remliel*. They work singly, and usually with one individual at a time. They learn of a soul's readiness for spiritual quickening through signals from a Watcher or Guardian Angel. From that moment forward, the Awakener gives unwavering attention to the candidate, a commitment consuming much of the Angel's activity. In doing so, there is no thought of exclusive interest or favoritism. Angelic motivation rises solely out of the will to prepare more individuals to serve God's Plan consciously as they themselves are doing.

Because this is the onset of the human being's realization of the spiritual path and his or her longing to aspire Godward, much of the Awakener's work comprises assisting the candidate in letting go of everything from outworn habits to resistant and rebellious attitudes. It is an ancient pattern when awakening to the Light, that finding it activates the individual's shadow side whose very existence is now placed in jeopardy. Paradoxically, it is in conquering the demons of one's instinctive nature that gives rise to the wisdom, skill, and resolve that every disciple needs in order to climb the Mountain of God. It is the actions of meeting and over-

coming the pitfalls of the personality self that open the gates of our own futures. The Remliel Angels perform for us an invaluable service to this end.

Frequently the Awakeners perceive, during a meditation, a group gathering, or an individual's testing, that a person requires definite assistance. Often they will be dealing with those who are new to the quest for God, but they also respond to other individuals who, while farther along the path, are in need of support and insight. In order to ready the probationer, disciple, or anyone who serves truth, these Angels make the best conditions possible for that soul's maturing. They first study the mentality of a student or novice to see by what means such an aspirant can be brought to surrender and conquer the resistant or destructive mind sets. They will bring to the attention of such individuals an array of information designed to activate insights through their own reflective study. Mental biases and instinctive complexes that issue from the personality's dark side can then be recognized, released, and healed. Destructive habits of thinking and acting left over from misadventures in previous lives often function as Achilles heels in our current incarnations. They crop up from emotional cores in the deep unconsciousness when we least expect them — unwelcome impulses that trip up our good intentions. When we lift these impulses prayerfully into the Light and make the sign of the cross in our Lord Christ's name, a cleansing takes place and we become purged of harmful energies.

Thus, individuals who apply themselves to the study of truth may, for a certain season, be overly self-conscious about their own inward purgation. When they understand that this is required and that very splendid, pure, and exceedingly intelligent Angel minds are guiding their footsteps, they will relax and work upon that which, by way of instruction, was unveiled during moments of self-revelation.

After this season of purification and self-revelation comes an opportunity for entering the arena of new mental growth. Recognizing that the unfinished business of human sediment is a continuing challenge, the Awakeners concentrate on what amounts to stretching and expanding the mental body so its currents and frequencies are steadily turned Godward. This affects one's intelligence and its various attributes, such as discernment, deduction, cognition, and memory. Such a period of choice and decision, wherein a disciple strives to achieve genuine dedication, marks a memorable crossroad in an individual's life.

Throughout their endeavors with their human candidates, the Awakeners focus on bringing all persons who can possibly be reached into the mental condition of *conscious spiritual return* — the condition of becoming aware of the Inner Worlds and the rich resources these contain. What facilitates this return is the fact that the incarnating humans are touching once again the shores of their eternal homeland. This requires consistent labor by the Remliel Angel in keeping the human recipient supplied with specific mental energies that cause the mental body to remain pure, flexible, eager, and intelligently enthusiastic.

In coming to the attainment of this condition of conscious spiritual return, two aspects of spiritual discipleship must work harmoniously together: illumination and self-conquest. Because of the confusion that we so often encounter between these seemingly opposing experiences, it will be helpful to clarify how they work together. As typically is the

case, the awakening to God is such a joyous and triumphant realization that, with it, comes a sense that from this point forward everything will be coming together in our lives. The truth is, the awakening itself is the realization of life's initial illumination with all of its attendant uplift. This is breaking through the barrier of being earth-bound and appreciating the transformation of consciousness invaded for the first time by the Presence of God.

It permanently changes our perception of life and reality in preparation of what lies ahead. As it is only the beginning of this archetypal journey, not its end, the hard work of self-conquest soon follows.

We discover, now that our eyes are open, that we must begin the arduous process of facing the truth about ourselves, much of which is neither flattering nor constructive. The Awakener Angels focus much of their attention on cleansing and purifying the human body, emotion, and mind. Since this is an undertaking that encompasses lifetimes, there is an inevitable crisis when our high hopes come crashing into the entrenched accumulation of unresolved and self-serving complexes that await conquest. It is not uncommon for each of us to feel overwhelmed or discouraged. But the time comes when we gain insight into this give-and-take relationship between our higher and lower natures and an equilibrium is restored. We come to expect progress akin to mountain climbing—for every obstacle overcome, there unfolds a grander view and a nearer awareness of the summit.

Awakeners, while committed to the purging process which makes room for enlightenment, also help to ready the mind for expanded receptivity to the higher frequencies of the Inner Worlds. What makes this such a promising development is the fact that it is the opening of the gates to insight, intuition, and creative perception. While in the past we too easily took pride in our own "giftedness," we now acknowledge that the gift we so quickly claimed comes to us from angelic mantling. What we can take credit for, if that is at all important, is making way for becoming more receptive and responsive to the extraordinary and inexhaustible Source that ultimately arises from the Creator.

What the Awakeners strive for is not so much the inspiration for great works of art or invention as the little beginnings of discipleship. These are demonstrated in the enlightening of consciousness and then the crafting of character.

Inspirers—the Angels of Wisdom

The next great order of Angels coming within notice of the novitiate is the host known as the *Inspirers* or, as they are called inwardly, the *Fireal*. These Angels of Wisdom are of an advanced rank and can only be contacted on the causal or soulic plane — a level far above ordinary human consciousness. Theirs is the ministry of inner quickening and revealing spiritual truths to those who are either in physical incarnation or attending one of the schools in the Inner Worlds.

They are most often associated with the governance of the arts and creativity for the most part. Yet, theirs is a larger work which deals with inspiring human beings to receive thoughts, incentives, vows, pledges, and spiritual steps beyond their own normal powers. The Inspirer Angels work

alone and they usually choose to aid an individual with whom they can remain in touch until a certain endeavor is concluded.

These Inspirers, as with all Angels serving the Holy Spirit, are constantly vigilant for opportunities to assist each of us in taking the next step of growth toward initiation and illumination. Great spiritual festivals such as Christmas, the New Year, Easter and Michaelmas are prime times for their mantling and prompting. Other personally significant occasions are an individual's birthday or the beginning of a new enterprise such as one's marriage or establishing a career or business.

It is at such times that we are most alive to promising possibilities and eager to learn new skills or venture into fresh fields of application, fanning into action flames of enthusiasm. What all of these spiritual milestones have in common is the greater openness and receptivity we present at such times. There are numerous other occasions when we are faced with a challenge or testing circumstance such as a final examination, a court appearance, a job interview, or any difficult assignment where cool headedness, courage, and centeredness in God are principal assets.

There is another time when we are particularly receptive to fresh impressions — when we travel, as on a spiritual journey to nature citadels, religious shrines, or cultural centers rich in artistic or humanitarian expression. When we travel, we are inclined to be more relaxed and expectant. Our auras are more porous and inviting of new impressions and realizations. At just such times as these, the Awakeners and the Inspirers are near at hand to lend their illuminating assistance.

94

Enlighteners

Thus far we have addressed how the Remliel and the Fireal work with humanity to quicken and purify their charges, as well as sponsor their creativity and bring them gifts of revelation. A still more transcendent endeavor is served by a company of Angels known as the *Enlighteners* or the *Imli*. Their principal work involves preparing individuals for the experience of initiation. As human evolution unfolds, there are five major thresholds that mark the ascent of the soul in the journey Godward. Each of these thresholds brings a transformation of the entire personality and the emergence of profound insights and capabilities. Each initiation ordinarily requires lifetimes for its attainment.

The Enlighteners work tirelessly to condition every human candidate to be worthy of these evolutionary milestones. Between each of these major initiations are countless minor initiations that form the stepping stones of daily growth. These can vary from simple insights that shed light on the answer to a problem, to significant awakenings revealing new dimensions of Truth.

While the minor initiations are the province of the Awakeners and the Inspirers, the Enlighteners center their attention on those who are candidates for crossing one of the five great initiatory thresholds. They can only be contacted in the region of humanity's highest, most unselfish, and most God-seeking thoughts and aspirations. As we have seen, the Awakeners focus especially on purifying their human charges by setting into motion the pursuit of self-conquest. The Inspirers focus on bringing their pupils to inner quickening and revelations of truth. The Enlighteners, in their

turn, concentrate their accelerating rays upon a novice who is ready for the bursting of self-bonds—always the prerequisite for the crossing of a major initiatory threshold.

Mountain heights are most favorable for communing with an Enlightener Angel. It is here that our ability is most conducive to soar in consciousness to those lofty heights where these extraordinary beings dwell. The capacity to make this connection coincides with the emergence of the soul becoming the dominant force in our lives. The personality self and its ego is at last beginning to fade into the background. With the emergence of the soul into consciousness come revelations into life's deeper mysteries as yet unknown to the candidate. What is particularly significant about crossing one of these thresholds is the onset of wisdom that accompanies it. And as with all manifestations of wisdom, it rings true.

There is about it a sense of timelessness as ancient as the sea, yet bearing the unique signature of originality that each candidate creates.

During this stage of our evolution, when there is growing rapport with the Angels serving the Holy Spirit, remarkable accomplishments in all fields of human activity take place. Great works of art, masterpieces of music and literature, new forms of government, education, religion, scientific discoveries, and a host of inventions and technological advances suddenly appear. Altogether, the quality of life is upgraded for entire nations and cultures. There are problems and unwelcome side effects, to be sure, but even these constructively challenge the ingenuity and enterprise of those affected and bring about even finer achievements.

Chohi

Above the Enlighteners are the *Chohi* who serve directly under the Holy Spirit. Their rank is equivalent to that of the Angels of the Christ Presence serving our Lord. Their work transcends the individual focus characteristic of those serving below them and centers, instead, upon world-changing movements whose effects are not only tremendously important but widespread, illuminating the age in which they occur. Their archetypes are fraught with the potency of the holy word. Sacred writings are chiefly the inspiration of the Chohi, as are all great movements and renowned accomplishments.

Humans, true to their earth-bound perspectives, too often fail to comprehend the origins of inspiration and creativity, taking for granted that this is a function of gifted individuals blessed with superior talents. In one respect, this is true. Such individuals indeed are gifted in their ability to tap into the thought frequencies initiated by the Chohi, or for that matter, any of the angelic orders serving the Holy Spirit. Nor is the channeling of a work inspired by such sources a passive act of slavishly recording a finished masterpiece. Oftentimes the respondent only captures a few highlights of the original transmission and what comes through may only partially resemble what was possible. There are, of course, many accounts of creative works that came wholly mantled, in which the respondent took no credit for the result. One thinks of Handel composing the Messiah or the chemist Kekule and his conception of the benzene ring in a dream-like reverie. It is well known that many of the great findings of science happened quite by accident when the

discoverer was rather aimlessly wandering about in an un-planned but receptive manner.

Arthur Koestler, in a book entitled *The Sleepwalkers*, de-scribed major breakthroughs in the history of astronomy as being made by gifted individuals doing what appeared to their contemporaries as illogical acts — behaving more like sleep-walkers following unconscious leads than rational scientists observing a disciplined methodology. With the Angels of the Holy Spirit in mind, one must envision these pathfinders as highly intuitive geniuses who were keenly receptive to inner promptings. Naturally, the established science of astronomy in any given age contains many misconceptions that obscure the yet-to-be-discovered truth. To break free of these ob-stacles, one must look in "unlikely" places, for the old knowl-edge stands squarely in the way of the new knowledge. Thus it is that creative people, whether in science, art, business, or child rearing, have the ability to get outside of themselves and listen to the inner voices of inspiration. As Koestler himself concluded, "The prerequisite of originality is to forget, at the proper moment, what we know."

How the Angels would rejoice if we humans had that abil-ity in abundance — to let go of our past misconceptions and prejudices and invite in the insights and realizations that signal our own futures.

Mystics of every age are the ones who best understand this divine mantling. Their very approach to the experience of higher states of consciousness directly links them with the Holy Spirit and the wondrous company of Angels serv-ing Him.

Mystics begin their quest for knowledge and divine wis-dom by going within. They commence their journey

Godward, as was said of Stephen in the New Testament, "full of faith and the Holy Spirit." The Lord Christ pointed the way when He said: "Neither say, lo here or lo there, for behold the Kingdom of God lies within you." With such a foundation the practice of mysticism holds great promise for the coming Aquarian Age.

In the chapter to follow we will present three remaining angelic orders that complete the principal ranks of these extraordinary beings who work closely with the human line of evolution. Two of these, the *Warrior Angels* and the *Amenlee Angels*, address the dark forces that put humanity to the test while the third, *Angels of Death*, conclude the orders serving the Angels of Destiny.

100

Warrior Angels, Amenlee Angels, and Angels of Transition

Both the Guardian and the Awakener Angels work diligently to help their human charges meet and overcome the dark side of human nature associated with the shadow and the testing elements that stand in the way of our spiritual advancement. When dealing with the resistant and often destructive forces characteristic of experiences we face in our human line of evolution, one of the constructive things we can do is to remember that these events test us. If we fail these encounters, we suffer the consequences. Hopefully, through the testing experience we learn a valuable lesson and are wiser for it. If we surmount the testing circumstances, we have sharpened and strengthened our skills of spiritual mountain climbing, earning the opportunity for further conquests. Otherwise, we will eventually face the test again and again, until we have mastered its lesson.

The Third Line of Evolution—the Demonic Path

Three paths of evolution mutually serve the goals of life's unfoldment. We are most familiar with our own line of human evolution and are becoming more aware of the second line, the angelic line of unfoldment. But we know far less about the third line, that of the demonic path. Its principal purpose is to tempt, challenge and compromise the efforts of all human subjects such that they will be negligent or untrue to their spiritual opportunities. As we recall, the archetypal encounter occurred with the Lord Christ in the wilderness when He was tempted three times by Satan. The classic response delivered by our Lord was "Get thee behind me, Satan." In a nutshell, that is the alpha and omega of our dealings with this force of evil.

We are tested at every turn as we strive Godward. As we are tested, the one response that always prevails absolutely is flat rejection of this line's cunning and deceptive stratagems. We must come to an enlightened degree of discernment so that we may recognize the entrapments the third line fashions for us. In our initial confrontations, we often are the victim rather than the victor. When we persevere and hone to a sharp edge our skills of detecting evil's hiding places, we soon find ourselves drawing even with and eventually surpassing this most formidable of adversaries.

The curious relationship the third line possesses with the human path is that as its forces are met and conquered by exemplary humans, the tempters actually regress, bit by bit, toward primal essence — the original stuff of which life is formed. Thus, theirs is a line of returning once again to the starting point of the evolutionary pathway. This ironic relationship means that in the long distance perspective of unfoldment Godward, there is actually cause for rejoicing for both the third line and human members when we overcome their testings. In no way, however, does this reduce the intensity or the duration of the force the third line brings to bear upon the human aspirant.

Known also as the anti-Christ, this force nevertheless plays a constructive role in the overall scheme of things. In a very real sense, it is the Mountain of God we must climb in our quest for self-mastery. All that challenges us in our daily duties, opportunities, and relationships also connects us with the beguiling and crafty ways of this dark intruder. While the Light is uncompromising in what it asks of us in facing this adversary; it is notably forgiving in the number of times we fall short of the mark in these encounters. How else could we humans finally season our skills and shape our strengths to gain victory?

It helps us greatly to realize we are not alone. Not only are there Guardian Angels and many hosts of radiant beings upon whom the Guardians can call, but one order in particular stands ready to do battle with the third line: the *Warrior Angels*. Serving under the Archangel Michael, this heroic, fearless, and vast company of Light Warriors has the glorious mission of scattering the forces of darkness and bringing forth the Light. This match invariably favors the Warrior Angels whenever the human will invokes their intervention. If the human will remains true to the Godward Path, all is well and the forces of darkness are turned away. Should the reverse be the case; should the human will compromise or cave in completely to the adversary's daring and deception leaving no foundation for the Archangel Michael and his Legions of Light Warriors to build upon, the result, as history records, will be disastrous. Worse still, not only will that particular battle be lost, but the impression will prevail that the forces of darkness are all-powerful. This disheartens many among the human line still struggling to be true.

It is at this point, when the impression looms large that evil is a dominant, irresistible power, that the Warrior Angels can perform their most effective work, for, as history also records, humanity survives. All that is needed is the willingness of even one soul on earth to seek their intervention through a determined stand against an encounter with evil. This is especially the case for those of us who have made a commitment to God to be of service and to live the Life. Our strength always will be tried. It is the age-old problem of proving our readiness and worthiness for what lies before us on the journey Godward. The Warrior Angels rejoice in being there to share in this engagement and eventual conquest.

Let's consider some of the characteristic elements that occur in encounters with evil. The more we know of this type of testing, the better equipped we will be to meet its force victoriously. When evil attacks, there is a numbing sensation and a period of bewilderment often bordering on panic. Yet, it is during this initial period of responding that the Light Legions work to strengthen our wills and ignite our engines of courage and resourcefulness. In effect, we are being transformed into warriors of the spirit and brought to a state of readiness that exceeds that of our adversary. The result is a combination of ability, agility, and fearlessness that will be more than a match for the testing powers.

As fear and the sense of vulnerability, which otherwise overwhelm us, wither away, we discover an ancient truth: with faith in God, all things are possible. It is then that we can meet the foe by being bold, trusting and calm — bold to protect our rights, trusting that Light is superior to darkness, and calm beneath the mantling of God's strength in the midst of the battle. Yes, the battle is hard, but the victory is enduring and splendid.

Whenever evil strikes, we need to have the assurance that we are never so alone or unprepared that we would imagine our position to be too imperiled. Those of the dark path are apt to act quickly in an attempt to wrest from us the prize or advantage desired while we are stunned. Given our weapons of inspired vigilance, insight, and faith in God, we will have the equal of their cunning and avarice. We should not act disturbed or fearful during such times of challenge. Instead, we should reveal a fighting spirit. Our warriorship is of and for the Light and our success lies in being undaunted, unafraid, and spiritually fortified on every plane of being.

In this great and noble cause, it is vital that we visualize the world of Light, the Warrior Angels, and all the vast resources that our Creator lays abundantly at our feet. We want to feel God's Presence ever in our midst, strengthening and empowering our wills to stand firm and true — feel ourselves as an extension of His supremacy over evil however it manifests. Above all, we must not underestimate or overestimate our enemy. Let us value our access to the world of Light and see this as our protection.

There is another important factor to mention when dealing with the third line. While it is true that we may hate, despise and oppose wrong doing or evil, we may *never* so regard persons. Nevertheless, when we are sure someone we know travels the path of evil, the wisest course of action is to accord this person indifference. Indifference, rather than hate, hurts these testers of humanity.

Thus far, we have focused most of our attention on our response to evil and how we can best protect ourselves. Let us now turn to the Archangel Michael himself, who is the source of much of our protection, along with his legions of Light Warriors.

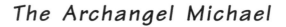

The Archangel Michael

First of all, his name "Michael" means *He who is of God.* And while his familiar title is that of Archangel, Flower learned that his true rank is that of an Angel Prince which is one step higher. He is mentioned in both the Old and New Testaments of the Bible. He is said to be the Angel of the Lord, referred to in Genesis, who restrained Abraham from offering his son Isaac as a sacrifice. Likewise, he is the one named in Revelations in the New Testament who hurled the dragon, Satan himself, from the heavens onto earth.

Three of the great world religions, Judaism, Christianity, and Islam, claim him as their protector. Earlier still, the Chaldeans looked upon him almost as a God and the ancient Egyptians chose him as their patron saint of the Nile. And closer to our times, Brittany and Cornwall both adopted him as their special Angel. The oldest shrine to Michael in England predates the establishment of the Christian church there.

The Archangel Michael and those who serve under him have extraordinary powers where evil and its perpetrators are concerned. Operating on the etheric plane, just above the physical world, they can actually disrupt and set back the schemes of those on earth who intend the triumph of evil. More significantly, where human selfishness, greed, and lust for power have created psychic cesspools of destructive energies, sometimes contaminating whole nations, these gallant Warriors tirelessly and fearlessly assail bastions of darkness, gradually purifying them.

Flower, who has seen the Archangel Michael, says that of all the Angels, his countenance is the most difficult for an artist to capture because it is constantly flashing, as if composed of lightning bolts. He is extremely tall, muscular, and powerfully built. The predominant color that radiates from his aura is orange, signaling his courage and immense strength.

While other Archangels are more expressive, he is wrapped in silence, even when most active. His authority and impact comes through his eyes which project flashing beams of light. One glance from him is sufficient to disrupt the intentions of evil or empower the intentions of the good. Both his hands and heart chakra also emit beams of light. When his arm is upraised above his head, these light beams become a sword commanding humanity to rise up from its instinctive origins and realize its spiritual destiny.

There is about him a divine fierceness befitting a Warrior of the Light whose task it is to pierce, disarm and transform evil. The fierceness defines the intensity of his focus in subduing an adversary that vigorously resists submission. What makes this task divine is that, in the end, it is an act of transformation rather than one of destruction. It is the nature of God's creativity that the dark powers putting humanity to the test are themselves purified by their confrontations with the Archangel Michael and his Light Legions. Faced with such potent weapons, it is logical to wonder how evil survives. Only one force keeps it alive: the human will succumbing to the enticements and temptations of the third line. Until that fatal weakness is overcome by the purifying of that same will, calamity is inevitable. It also follows that once it is overcome, evil will wither away and disappear. It is what the Lord Christ meant when He said, "Thy kingdom come, Thy will be done, on earth as it is in heaven." What remains for each of us is the fulfillment in our own lives of that reality.

There is a wonderful record of this magnificent Angel Prince in the life of Joan of Arc. This humble, innocent peasant girl — the unlikeliest of warrior material — came out of obscurity to lead the armies of France to a great victory. When her enemies contrived a case against her and she was brought to trial as a witch, she was asked whether or not she actually saw the Archangel Michael along with other Angels. St. Joan answered, "I saw them with my bodily eyes as well as I see you, and when they left me, I … would have them take me with them, too."

The Archangel Michael is one of four great Angels best known in the Christian faith who sponsor the work of the Lord Christ. Another of these great Angels is the Archangel Gabriel who announced the birth of Jesus and who remained in charge of an epoch that lasted until the Renaissance. He watched over the establishment of the church and the age of faith. With the beginning of the Renaissance in Italy, the Archangel Raphael headed an awakening of discoveries in basic science and the unfoldment of artistic creativity and splendor until our present 20th century.

The Archangel Michael is in charge of our present era and will retain this commission until around 2500 A.D. This mighty Angel Prince is needed in our troubled times, for he is a Warrior who does battle with fiendish forces that have vented themselves upon our world in distortions of appetites, of sex, of morality, and of crime and war. He will bring humanity to reestablished order, law, and self-control through spiritual means. He, in turn, will be succeeded by the Archangel Uriel who is pledged to an enlightened era of philosophy and a futuristic science.

It needs to be emphasized that the Archangel Michael's battleground is not only against evil as it manifests in the world around us, but as well in the world within each of us. It is in the activation and misdirection of our personal shadow, that undercuts our good intentions and precipitates the dark side of our human nature; be that of fear, anger, greed, pride or whatever. Of the two arenas where we face manifestations of evil, it is the shadow within that makes us most vulnerable and at risk. And it is in overcoming the shadow through its transformation that gives us the most protection from the effects of evil as it appears in the external world around us.

It is also the means that brings about our own unfoldment Godward.

The Archangel Michael and his Light Legions, while possessing overwhelming strength to neutralize evil, nevertheless depend upon us to open the gates of our beings for their entrance. Otherwise, evil would have long ago been vanquished from the earth. It is our efforts to overcome our own inferior attributes that provides these Light Warriors the opportunity to assist us. This commitment of constructive endeavor on our part links us with these valiant beings to gain the conquest.

One of the great paradoxes in the quest for God is the fact that when we finally awaken to His Presence in our lives and we find ourselves making vows and life rules, the favorite weapon the human shadow employs is neglect. We simply forget about their existence. So it is with these mighty

Angels when we neglect to summon them to deal with evil wherever it strikes. They can only respond to those of us on earth who recognize their reality and call upon them to take action. God is almighty. Evil poses no threat to the immensity of Creation. It is the human path of evolution and its exercising of free will that allows Light here on earth to be opposed and neglected, or championed.

Much of our encounter with evil lies in the backlog of negative karma that plays a key role in the onset of trials and testing circumstances associated with this path. This accounts for much of the outbreak of violence and tragic destruction that befalls humanity for no apparent reason. What counts in either case is our positive, enlightened, self-conquering response to all of life's challenges that otherwise discourage, divide, and defeat us. So positioned, we have behind us the victorious presence of Archangel Michael ready at a moment's notice to make all the difference in the outcome of any confrontation with darkness.

One final thought about the habits of these mighty presences that gives insight into their preferences in times of repose. Angels have abodes in the Inner Worlds where they go for renewal and further enlightenment. Flower once described her visit to such a retreat for Warrior Angels. It was on an astral plane (just above the physical and etheric planes) in a setting of nature. There was a palisade of great boulders and from out of this massive wall of stone plunged a magnificent waterfall. To one side was a field filled with many beautiful flowers and fragrances. Seeing a light-filled grotto, Flower entered it. Just outside its opening stood a tree resembling a giant sequoia. Nearby was a Warrior Angel looking up at a most unusual luminous essence in the form of a shining fountain. All through this experience she could hear the constant sound of angelic voices singing what reminded her of Wagner's *Cry of the Valkyries*.

Amenlee Angels

Closely related to the Warrior Angels is the order of the *Amenlee*. Their work is with rebellious members of humanity known as the *incorrigibles*. These are the strongly self-willed personalities who provoke all types of challenges to wholesomely evolving human beings. This brings up the chief distinction between the evolution of Angels and that of the human race: Angels progress through their *works*, whereas humans move Godward by means of *self-surrender*. The more works Angels victoriously achieve, the readier they are for higher degrees of initiation. In turn, the more self-surrendered humans become, the closer they draw to their own initiatory thresholds.

The Amenlee belong to the Angels of Destiny and they hold the same advanced rank as Guardian Angels or Warrior Angels. They work closely with advanced angelic orders who serve the Holy Spirit. Most humans in their inevitable dealings with evil receive incentives toward voluntary changes from those who form the ranks of these illumined beings. Within themselves, humans wage battles between what are called their lower and higher natures. In this creative conflict they are given insights and self-revelations from the Holy Spirit. Unfortunately, not everyone holds to the normal path of unfoldment and tragic exceptions occur among those who are rebellious in nature, resulting in harm to both themselves and others.

After a Guardian Angel along with an Angel serving the Holy Spirit have studied these erring individuals and found them closed to spiritual influences, an Amenlee Angel is summoned. This one thoroughly examines the inversion of pride that underlies such cases, including a study of their virtues and weaknesses, then acts upon the perverse will in any of several ways. An Amenlee may choose to bring the rebel into the society of spiritually strong souls, or into close companionship with persons of wholesome backgrounds whose wills are aligned to the good. The time given to such a study of an individual, of course, varies with each person. Those who have been afflicted with destructive and willful habits, yet whose temperaments are fundamentally sound and responsive, are often transformed by exampleship alone.

If an individual under consideration still remains unmoved and uninfluenced by this initial treatment, the Amenlee Angel may bring about an introduction of the rebel to teachers of powerful development or of unusual spirituality. There are wonderful stories told of the work of Father Flanagan, a Catholic priest, who founded Boys Town in Nebraska in 1917.

He was famous for the statement, "There is no such thing as a bad boy." The boys he took in included many who were at odds with the law or who were runaways from unhappy homes. His success in reaching these often angry and defiant youths using strict discipline, combined with respect and deep caring, is legendary. Clearly, he was a channel for the Amenlee order.

If the rebel's reaction is still unfavorable, then entirely new and exciting events are precipitated. These cases match extreme circumstances with extreme attitudes. They characteristically involve what amounts to a form of shock therapy designed to get the individual's attention and hopefully achieve a turnaround. A case in point, although fictional, is the character Jean Valjean in Victor Hugo's novel, *Les Miserables*. While not a rebel in the beginning, after being imprisoned for a number of years for stealing a loaf of bread to feed his starving family, he is embittered and ruled by anger. He subsequently is befriended by a trusting priest, only to steal the holy man's silver service. Captured and brought before the priest again, Valjean is stunned to hear the priest insist that the silver was a gift, and in fact, to be offered additional pieces he had "overlooked." The impact of this extraordinary and unexpected kindness profoundly changes Valjean's whole attitude and he sets out to become a model citizen. Certainly this process of transmutation has many counterparts in real life that go unnoticed, except to the administering Angels.

For more serious cases, only testing of an increasingly severe kind can confront a rebel with the imperative prerequisites of change. The Amenlee Angel, after an interim, restudies the case, noting how deeply the human charge has been affected by trying, humiliating or sorrowful experiences.

Sometimes when severely tested, rebels who have been unaffected by other measures acquiesce to their urgent need for self-surrender.

Those remaining few who are abnormally unresponsive are recognized to be in a very serious plight. When more than one lifetime has passed under the watchful striving of an Amenlee Angel to wrest an individual's soul from the abyss of insanity or criminality, it brings that person to a crossroads. It now becomes clear that the soul in question is definitely choosing to be aligned with inhuman, demonic intelligences. At this juncture, the Amenlee involved will summon more advanced, more experienced Amenlee Angels to survey his work and to suggest new modes of attack. Thus commences a renewed assault under the watchful eye of this senior Amenlee to rescue the endangered soul.

This concerted effort involves an infusion of fresh elements intended to stir a new awakening, intermingled with many of the earlier types of circumstances. The innovations introduced at intervals, along with the presence of an advanced Amenlee Angel not previously experienced, create a sense of newness that, to a limited extent, may capture the attention of the recalcitrant rebel.

Yet there are individuals so insensitive, so inhumanly bound to delusions of self-importance, that they are unmoved by these valiant endeavors. The advanced Amenlee may appeal to Archangels serving with the Angel Prince Michael to engage their superior forces against the gathering darkness within this soul's unbending state of mind.

Only a scant number of humans among the incorrigibles remain totally unresponsive to all these approaches wholeheartedly administered by the Angel kingdom. For these entrenched few there is one last court of appeals — the Spirit of Grace and Mercy.

This aspect of the Godhead brings an entirely new energy and focus to the situation. Through this Host, selfless service is administered in a mysterious way that transcends our human observation or comprehension. In this final effort on behalf of the rebel, exalted angelic presences of infinite compassion take upon themselves a certain degree of responsibility for this one's evolution. They perform work for the incorrigible that is wholly beyond the will or merit of this individual.

In spite of all these interventions, there still exist some few human incorrigibles. These are the sad ones approaching the boundary between two worlds — the human and the demon. They appear to be creatures devoid of human feeling, whose only emotion is sadistic or demonic because they are nearing that stage of inhuman intelligence. Only rarely are souls unable to be saved by the all-encompassing, tender and merciful love of the Spirit of Grace and Mercy. The handful of these hapless individuals who join the ranks of the destructive line of evolution have proved strangely and stubbornly unfit for the human way of voluntary self-surrender to the Eternal God.

Yet these beings, once they have deliberately chosen evil as their path, will inexorably continue regressing, eventually to be returned to primal essence. Purified at last they can begin anew with the process of human evolution.

The Angels of Death or Transition

Finally, we turn to the last group of Angels in this chapter — the *Angels of Death or Transition*. Chapter three included a description of the Angels of Birth who watch over our entrance into human incarnation.

Angels of Death are the ones who return us to our true Homeland. They belong to the Angels of Destiny and can either be male or female. According to our karmic destiny, governed by a key in our life graph, the time comes for each one of us to conclude our incarnation. At such a moment the Angels of Death administer an electrical force which severs the inner bodies from the physical form and brings about the condition known as death. While we on earth often associate deep feelings of loss or sadness with this event, it is with wonder and joy that one returns to the Inner Worlds.

On returning, the first realization of which we are aware is that of engulfing Light and the first being we observe is the wonderfully compassionate Angel of Transition. Of Archangel rank, this presence of unspeakable beauty and outshining love gently welcomes each one of us to this long forgotten dimension of existence. As we gradually recall our true Homeland, we wonder how such a familiar and perfect world could ever be forgotten.

Before this time of remembrance reawakens, the Angel of Transition brings each soul returning to the Inner Worlds to a series of three pools. The first is the Pool of Cleansing. Its color is composed of soft blue radiations. Those wading into this pool notice a tingling penetration of charged elements stimulating their senses. Because its waters have positive electrical polarity, this pool releases the astral body of its tensions and negative currents. Through this beneficial cleansing, individuals come to recognize their freedom and new identity.

The second pool is the Pool of Peace, whose waters are a luminous blue tone, more vivid than those of the first pool. The Angels of Transition direct the newly returned souls to give themselves individually to these waters which bathe

the recipients in special gifts and benedictions from these great Angels.

This experience leaves us with the feeling best described as "the peace of God which passeth all understanding."

The third pool is the Pool of Renewal. It has a blue-green emanation and is receptive to certain frequencies of the Spiritual Sun. From this pool, individuals gain contact with a wellspring of constant energy which remains with them throughout their existence in the Inner Worlds. It is an energy well exceeding the earthly equivalent of the best of our healthiest, most active years.

After passing through the three pools, significant aspects of each soul's incarnation are reviewed. This includes not only one's accomplishments but the mistakes and transgressions as well. It is necessary for the soul to actually experience the hurt he or she may have caused in another person's life, whether it was intentional or out of carelessness. The Angel of Transition keeps in contact with the returning individual until the completion of his or her memorial service. Then at last, reunion with relatives and friends takes place.

Flower recalls two experiences with the Angels of Transition that were particularly memorable. The first occurred when her grandmother crossed over into God's World. Flower and her husband Lawrence were present with her in her hospital room. Suddenly it appeared to Flower that the room lights were flickering and she mentioned this to Lawrence. He answered that neither he nor an aunt who was also present noticed anything unusual. Then Flower realized that on levels higher than outer eyes could see, the death experience was beginning to unfold. For her the room grew brighter and brighter until with a blinding flash, the Light vanished altogether. It was at this moment that they realized her grandmother was gone and that only her frail body remained.

Before the Light had grown too bright to witness, Flower had observed a very tall feminine figure of an Angel smiling down upon her grandmother. She seemed to be communicating encouragement and welcome to this loved one. Flower commented that she would never forget the beauty and the love on the face of this Angel of Death. "How wonderful it must be," she said, "to step free of one's worn out body into such love and compassion."

The second experience took place in 1967 and was most remarkable. The setting was in Buenos Aires, Argentina, while Flower was leading some thirty-five travellers on a spiritual journey to South America. The weather had been stormy, and after several delays, the group finally found themselves aboard an aircraft bound for Bariloche in Argentina's lake region. The pilot, however, was visibly upset over orders to fly in such weather. Flower, sensing danger, felt prompted to gather her group together and disembark. The captain impatiently refused permission and gunned the propeller-driven aircraft down the taxi runway in preparation for takeoff. Glancing out of the window, Flower was startled to see several Angels of Death carefully observing their plight. It was then she realized the gravity of their situation and knew that something terrible was about to happen. Just then the pilot, having overshot the runway, slammed on the brakes, causing the plane to skid out of control and veer off the concrete surface. As the landing gear on the aircraft's port side sank into the mud, it collapsed, forcing the wing to plunge downward and driving the engines into the ground. Instantly, one of the propellers tore loose from its shaft and slashed through the cabin, missing Flower's son Galen by inches. Mercifully, nothing caught fire and the ill-fated craft came to a lurching halt.

What impressed Flower most about this episode, next to their safe delivery from tragedy, was the fathomless compassion in the countenances of these tall, loving Angels of Death. She would remember throughout the rest of her life the wonder of their comforting presences. It gave new meaning to the Apostle Paul's words, "O death, where is thy sting? O grave, where is thy victory?"

Communing with Angels

124

In fulfilling her mission to reveal and honor the Angel Kingdom, Flower intended more than a compilation of knowledge about these extraordinary beings. Above all else, she intended that we *experience* their reality, so that through that experience we would be able to benefit from their influence and instruction.

Our quest to experience the reality of Angels is aided by our longing for enlightenment and for drawing closer to God. This is the saving grace of our spiritual hunger and thirst, which keeps us striving on the path of becoming fit and worthy. Working against us, however, are two conditions. The first is the demanding presence of the physical world, ever suggesting this plane is the one and the only reality. God, His Angels, and the Inner Worlds, being invisible to most people, easily go unnoticed and therefore unremembered. It requires a conscious, enduring act of faith to keep the vision of these realities alive in the face of the world's intrusiveness.

The second obstacle to be dealt with, and in many ways the more formidable one, is the human shadow — the primitive, instinctual, and dark side of the human personality. Of this entrenched opponent of the Light, the Apostle Paul said: "The good that I would, I do not, and the evil that I would not, that I do." The Guardian and Awakener Angels are aware of the shadow and its hold on our appetites and choices; that is precisely why they focus so much of their attention on alerting us to overcoming the negativities of our lower nature.

When we recognize conditions that either assist or challenge our approach to Angels, our desire is to build a bridge of communion with them. The vehicle which makes this construction possible is the development of inner perception, the sixth sense.

This in itself is a fascinating adventure; it opens gates not only to the Angel Kingdom, but also to God and the Inner Worlds.

The Role of Intuition

The threshold leading to this illuminating ability is human intuition. If we stop for a moment and reflect on how our minds take in experience and all the information it yields, we will realize, along with the renowned Swiss psychologist, Carl Jung, that this happens in two different ways. The first modality is direct sensory input; the second is indirectly, through the voice of intuition.

Jung called the direct mode *sensation*. Obviously, sensation is very concrete, down to earth, and practical. Its connection is solidly with the earth and its physical properties, usually referred to as the five senses.

Jung termed the indirect mode of mental processing *intuition*, or what is often termed the sixth sense. This quality is illuminating, insightful, and creative. Intuition connects with the world of possibilities, implications, and imagination.

Clearly, intuition is the natural vehicle for receiving impressions, realizations, and revelations. It reads between the lines, grasps significances, and communes with other worlds. It is indeed the gateway to inner perception. As this is the principal means of contacting Angels, the wise unfoldment of this capability is an important goal.

The term "wise unfoldment" needs to be understood. There is a certain fascination and glamorous excitement that frequently surrounds the idea of contacts with invisible realities, sometimes accompanied by a magical or supernatural setting. When this becomes fascination with phenomena and the unusual for its own sake, it loses its spiritual value and turns into a sensational and oftentimes overdramatized, exploitative, and even dangerous exercise.

At its worst, this is open to trickery and abuse. Even at its best, with honorable intentions, what comes through may be little more than wishful thinking or idealistic speculation.

The Sincere Desire to Do God's Will

The foundation for communing with Angels, then, is based on a sincere desire to do God's will through contact with this kingdom, and to awaken our sixth sense faculties constructively. There can be no better beginning than to be well-informed about Angels. A number of books have appeared recently on this subject. As they differ in many ways, trust your intuition to guide you to those works and those aspects of each book that ring true for you.

Certainly, one of the first and finest connections we can make is contact with our Guardian Angel. It is she who is truly our spiritual mother, and she who remains with us longer than any other Angel presence of any type. Without her help, we human beings would seldom achieve sustained spiritual interest or possess courage for making spiritual growth.

A quintessential skill to unfold is remembrance of the reality of the Angels, and a gradual sensitivity to their impressions and instruction. Although each person will need

127

to develop his or her best approach to this practice, the following suggestions have proven helpful to others.

The Habit of Remembrance

An important discipline in this quest is to establish the habit of remembrance and tuning in. This can best be accomplished by making a commitment — a spiritual vow, if you will — that is carried out on a regular basis.

It is very helpful to keep a spiritual journal with a record of the vow and consistent daily evaluation of its progress. State your vow in specific language, so that it is clear what exactly you intend to accomplish. For example, you might write, "I will turn my thought to the presence of Angels about me at least four times a day. Each time I will note any impressions that come to me." Then record each day's fulfillment, or lack of it, along with observations of what took place or how you might improve your experience.

In this exercise it is the quality of remembrances that is most important, not their sheer quantity. Quality will be largely reflected in the nature of your consciousness during the periods of remembrance. If your attitude remains resistant or skeptical, you will score a minus. If it is routine, dutiful, but uninspired, you will score a zero. If it is uplifting, perhaps wrapped in a sense of wonder, you will score a plus. An especially illuminating insight would score a double plus.

A sample journal entry might take the following form:

	Quantity		Quality	Comments
	Yes	no	- *0* +	
Period 1		✔	-	*Overslept*
Period 2	✔		*0*	*Routine*
Period 3	✔		+	*Better, had insight*
Period 4	✔		+ +	*Felt a powerful presence*

In using any recording system, make sure it does not become mechanical or so routine it is no longer helpful.

A period of four to six weeks (for instance, the Lenten season preceding Easter, or Advent in preparation for Christmas) is a practical time frame for establishing a change in one's attitudes or habit patterns. At the end of the six weeks, if this method is no longer beneficial, a new approach would be in order.

Flower often cautioned her students that one should never expect dramatic or extraordinary results. The awakening of inner perception is a gradual transformation, like the dawning of a new day. It should unfold by degrees and should never be pursued aggressively or ambitiously.

Because phenomena are prized in certain quarters of our thrill-loving culture, there is a danger of becoming caught up in an atmosphere of such suggestibility that forces visions which are similar to hypnotically induced visions. It is essential that we approach the Angels fully conscious, purely motivated, free of any desire to impress or amaze others.

One more cautionary note: it is common to all paths leading to enlightenment that once a seeker is in earnest, the human shadow makes its move to ignore, divert, or shut down the effort. It is the great paradox of the journey Godward that the awakening to the Light is the event that engages the shadow in an archetypal holy war. Yet it is this very engagement that generates the resolution, the skills, and the conditioning to complete the journey.

The shadow's principal weapon is often simply to cause us to neglect our good intentions. The result is that we pronounce our vows of remembrance only to forget to recall them. Another device used by the shadow is fault-finding. We begin to consider this discipline to be an inconvenience, a burden, a source of conflict. Sooner or later, we start resisting the endeavor, and that brings an end to our effort.

In dealing with the shadow, we must never give in to its diversions. As often as necessary, we must persevere and start afresh. At first, we may not register noticeable progress. What counts, however, is our determination not to let the shadow prevail. It is important to remember that we are not wholly at its mercy, for the soul within each of us is more than its match. Given enough time, the soul will always triumph.

Drawing Closer to Angels Through Nature

For our drawing closer to the Angel kingdom, nature provides an ideal setting. This is particularly so if one enters it alone. Finest of all is a mountain wilderness that can be reached by an ascending trail. Here amidst its scenic grandeur we can brush away the cobwebs of uninspired thought and feel the pure, invigorating currents of nature's aliveness seeping into our very souls. Approach an inviting viewpoint or lean against a lofty tree, then quietly bring yourself to a state of welcoming receptivity. With journal or notebook in hand, write down any thoughts or realizations that come your way. Again, these need not be great revelations. Record any openings and insights that lift your consciousness and enrich your appreciation of life.

If you do not have access to a mountain wilderness, seek out whatever is available in its place. Even city parks or backyard gardens offer upliftment, particularly if you can spend time there alone and free from interruptions.

Angels in Places of Worship

Angels also seek out places of worship and consecration. Everything from humble prayer chapels to great cathedrals attract those beings who revere the holiness present in such places. In addition, shrines that honor great souls often are power centers for angelic presences. The Lincoln Memorial in Washington, D.C. is such a consecrated edifice. Over this tribute to our greatest president abides a most magnificent presence known as the *National Angel*.

In Italy, the entire city of Assisi attracts numerous Angels who serve the Christ. As you recall, it was St. Francis who rescued Christianity from the machinations of the politics of the middle ages and reinfused the holiness of Christ into the consciousness of the church. Another place of angelic power is located in New Delhi, India, at the memorial for Mahatma Gandhi.

There are many others, often found in byways free from the press of crowds. As part of your increasing awareness, practice coming to stillness within a quiet temple or shrine. In this stillness you may be able to discern the flow of energy from inner presences. Ask yourself these questions— What are the predominant characteristics of this place? Do you sense a presence? Is there a feeling, a keynote phrase, a color, or musical tone that comes through to your consciousness? Again, record your impressions in your spiritual journal. With time, your sensitivities will become so increased that you will be readily open to communing with the Angels.

Communing with Angels Through the Arts

Great works of art can be an inviting force for the Angel Kingdom. Leonardo da Vinci's painting of the Last Supper and Michaelangelo's statue of David have this effect. Many art galleries, where the paintings on exhibit genuinely reflect the sanctity or nobility of their subjects, also ray out energies that summon the Angels. Not only do the Angels delight in the uplift of the auric radiations surrounding such masterpieces, but these glorious presences return a baptism of inspiration to the gallery visitors, that, to a sensitive recipient, can be profoundly moving. So it is that the Angels drawn to such exhibits find this to be a door-opening opportunity to arouse dor-

132

mant wonder, or ignite the fires of holy enthusiasm, with their human counterparts.

Guardian Angels are particularly appreciative of these opportunities to stir the hearts of their charges. Whole new awakenings, strivings and changes can then begin in the lives of the humans who have been so stirred.

Music is another pathway that generates energies to touch the hearts of those of us on earth who long for a connection with the Inner Worlds. Listening to a great symphony, magnificent opera, or masterful concerto can transport us into higher realms of consciousness. Music wraps around us, seeps within us, and brings us to thresholds of upliftment and transport that no other medium duplicates. Unlike paintings or sculptures, which are frozen in time, music unfolds and has a life of its own within the listener.

Hal A. Lingerman, who has published insightful and informative books on this subject[*] has written entire chapters on music inspired by angelic beings.

He has spent many years as an associate minister with Flower at Questhaven Retreat. Flower worked with Hal to add significant insights and inner observations to his research. He cites over fifty pieces in his chapter on Angelic Music in *The Healing Energies of Music*, including such sublime classics as the *Hallelujah Chorus* from Handel's *Messiah*, *Panis Angelicus* by Franck, Mahler's

---

[*] Hal A. Lingerman, *The Healing Energies of Music*, Quest Books, Wheaton, Il, 1983.
Hal A. Lingerman, *Life Streams, Quest Books*, Wheaton, Il, 1988.

Symphony No. 2 (Resurrection), and Wagner's *Ride of the Valkyries.*

What channels such musical masterpieces is the sixth sense of a composer who is sufficiently awakened to capture strains of the Music of the Spheres. As the Inner Worlds are alive with light and color, so are they dynamic with sound and music. From this bountiful source comes an endless procession of melodies, themes, and choruses broadcast by Angels of Music praising God and His Creation.

There was, of course, before the advent of recording, a time when music needed to be freshly recreated to be enjoyed. Now with the advances in recording technology, everyone can hear exquisite music, with nearly perfect fidelity, as often as desired. Although the nobility of previous eras could and did commission music for their purposes, not even kings could command the luxury of inspired music performed flawlessly each time. The creative energies of music now provide for all of us a readily accessible royal road into the Angel kingdom.

Another of the art forms that summons the Angels is the dance. When performed with reverence, joy, and an outpouring of universal love, the dance becomes a form of worship attracting these heavenly visitors. Classic examples are works such as Tchaikowsky's Swan Lake, or the artistry of Nijinsky or a Pavlova.

In many of the religions of antiquity, sacred temple dancers wove their movements into prayers directed toward Divinity. Flower herself remembered being a temple dancer during her previous lives in both Egypt and Greece. At Questhaven Retreat, she has incorporated this form of worship as an integral part of its program, especially at the high retreats of Michaelmas, Christmas, Easter and the Summer Solstice.

The expressiveness and creativity of the spiritual dance movement is beginning to open doors in several other innovative churches as well. Given the close link between the presence of Angels where there is an atmosphere of reverence and consecration, and the grace and beauty of dancers symbolically recreating the movement and uplift of angelic hosts, this form of expression becomes a natural bridge between their world and ours.

Finally, we have the art forms of both the spoken and written word. In her day, there was no more ardent, eloquent, or moving spokesperson for the Angels than Flower. Whenever she spoke of their kingdom, it was as their champion. The sense of wonder and holiness in her voice touched the hearts of all her listeners.

What was most unique about Flower was the simple fact that what she had to say about the Angels was from her direct knowledge. Through her gift of clairvoyance, she saw them just as freely and naturally as we see each other.

She was not speculating, or imagining, or making inferences from things she had read or heard others say. She saw (and heard unobstructedly) into the Angel's dimension of existence. Thus, her descriptions of Angels along with her revelations about their various orders, activities, and destinies form a rich legacy for present and future generations.*

The written word casts a broader net, as there are many records of Angels in the world's literature. Besides their

* Both audio & videotapes of her lectures on the subject of Angels are available from the Christward Ministry.

numerous appearances in both the Old and New Testaments, and the extraordinary Books of Enoch, Angels feature prominently in the Apocrypha, the writings of William Blake, Geoffrey Hodson, Emmanuel Swedenborg, Thomas Aquinas, Jacob Boehme and many others. Yet of all of these, the most clearly descriptive and inclusive commentary of Angels in their native habitat comes from Flower's two volumes, *Rediscovering the Angels* and *Kingdom of the Shining Ones*.

Beyond writings on the Angels themselves is the rich field of literature whose stories and characterizations stir to life the longings and strivings of its readers toward great causes and noble acts. The novels of the Bronte sisters and Charles Dickens possess these qualities. A sampling of titles that would be welcomed by the Angels includes such nonfiction works as William James' *Varieties of Religious Experience*, Raynor Johnson's *Watcher on the Hills*, and Madeline L'Engles' *Walking on Water*. Among fiction, Lew Wallace's *Ben-Hur,* and *The Robe* by Lloyd C. Douglas stand out, along with the novels of Graham Greene, those of Pearl Buck, and such mythical tales as C. S. Lewis' *Chronicles of Narnia*. Playwrights, too, leave a legacy of angelic inspiration, from the Greeks through Shakespeare, and continuing into contemporary drama. The vast world of poetry, ranging from the Psalms of David to the lyrics of Oscar Hammerstein, also touches the angelic worlds.

Indeed, the list of books that have opened the doors of consciousness, revealed new horizons, touched hearts, and altogether changed lives is beyond count. This very fact illuminates why the Angels carefully observe us as we enjoy these works of art. They wait for us to reach a particular passage or respond to a given character in a manner that opens us, allowing them to imprint their connection in our auras.

Whenever anything makes a deep impression upon us, whether while experiencing an art form, in the midst of a human relationship, or venturing forth on a nature outing, we can be sure an Angel is involved. This is one of the tell-tale signs of their presence—one of their favorite ways of getting our attention. In this way, they can touch our lives with newness, freshness and soul-stretching growth.

138

Angels Touching Us

140

Angels—Guardian Angels in particular—can send us impressions, realizations, intuitive insights, and inner promptings. Indeed, until our sixth sense is fully unfolded and we have direct contact with this kingdom, those are the principal ways they touch us. These experiences typically come to us unexpectedly. Suddenly, the thought or realization appears in our heads and there it is, ready or not, like it or not. On occasion, the influence of an Angel takes another form and will manifest in the development of a situation or an encounter with another individual or group. We can be sure that, however they choose to call things to our attention, they are marvelously resourceful in getting through to us. They have one inviolate rule: they never interfere with our freewill. The Angels can instruct us, remind us, inspire us, or present us with challenging circumstances, but it is we, as human aspirants, who make the final choice.

To some, this may seem inefficient and wasteful inasmuch as we humans are so error prone and divided in our loyalties. Would it not be simpler to have God instruct us directly and save all of these mistakes and wrong decisions? Yet it is God's design of human evolution that individuals learn through the consequences of their actions. In other words, across lifetimes and in the pattern of our choices, we are the authors of our own circumstances. We can no longer blame fate or misfortune.

An Angel's Priorities

High among the priorities of our Guardian Angel, as well as the Awakener Angel representing the Holy Spirit, is going after our personality's dark side. This is a vital step, since

up to now we have been tolerant of our lapses into darkness, our self-centeredness, our laziness, and the many outworn habits and attitudes that hold us back.

The time must come when we awaken to a longing to leave behind us the enticing and self-indulgent shadows of the past. What must be ignited in its place is the quest for enlightenment, for the refinement and strengthening of character, and for our becoming self-emptied and God-filled.

Self-centeredness and insincerity, to an Angel, are two of the most repellent aberrations found in human nature. The thought of putting self before God is inconceivable to one of their company. It is the absolute antithesis of a life of service. Insincerity likewise is unknown in their world. To put on appearances, to mislead, to give false impressions, to say one thing when we mean another, constitutes a fault of such magnitude that our progress is greatly impeded, standing in the way of our access to the angelic kingdom.

There is a classic pattern to the encounter between the shadow and the soul. After too many lifetimes of compromise and living in the moral twilight between truth and the deception of worldly pursuits and temptations, there comes a breakthrough. Sometimes it is as gradual as the gathering light of dawn. Other times it takes us by surprise, like a bolt out of the blue. However it comes, it transforms us so that we at last see our direction and our destiny. With this, a feeling stirs to life that we are seeing the light. Along with this illumination comes the extraordinarily optimistic attitude that henceforth all will be well. In the words of the poet Robert Browning, "God's in His heaven and all's right with the world."

In our unbridled enthusiasm for the joys of the awakening, we are likely to mistake the beginning of the journey

142

for its conclusion. Yes, at long last we have found the way, but ahead of us lies the Mountain of God which has yet to be climbed. Its challenges and demands are formidable, just as its revelations and rewards are without equal.

There are some early skirmishes with the shadow before the emerging disciple finally recognizes that this is not cause for disillusionment or abandonment. Instead, it is a call to commitment, self-conquest, and the steadfast desire for the experience of God.

It is especially during this period that both the Guardian Angel and the Awakener Angel bring to our attention the outcroppings of our unfinished business. Our Guardian Angel, who best understands where our next step of growth is needed, carefully observes the condition of our readiness and formulates a plan of action. She then brings us to an awareness of our needs, sometimes through a clear realization blooming in our minds, other times by arranging an encounter with circumstances that bring us to terms with ourselves. Either way, with her help, we take on the task of transformation.

The Joy of the Guardian Angel

Flower underscored the significance of our victories in these matters. Nothing we can do matches the joy and delight of the Guardian or Awakener Angel when we at last let go of an unworthy trait or mistaken notion. Its conquest reverberates throughout the Inner Worlds; celebrating the advance of one more human by one more step up the ladder of evolution.

The onset of the awakened soul marks the beginning of an adventure that will not conclude until one's earthly evo-

lution is complete. Flower, in one of her earliest writings, called it the *School of Life*. In this, she compared our passages across lifetimes to grades in a school.

There are lessons to be learned, examinations to be passed, and standards to be met. The lessons that we fail will need to be repeated over and over until we finally master them. Those who progress constructively from grade to grade will know the reward of fulfillment and the sense of wellbeing that comes from the attainment of a worthy goal.

Over the years at Questhaven Retreat, we have seen a pattern of response emerge that is both consistent and informative. An individual, after years of wandering, discovers Christian mysticism and all of its revelations of the Inner Worlds, the Hierarchy of Perfected Souls, the Angel kingdom, reincarnation and karma, discipleship, and the path of initiation and illumination that leads to mastery. So transforming is this experience, so revolutionary is its impact, that the person feels utterly reborn and in possession of the secrets of the universe. This soul identifies absolutely with the truth of these realities. To this person, knowledge equals attainment. Then by one means or another comes the painful realization that there is a huge gap between simple knowledge of truth and its application and fulfillment in life. Often, many lifetimes of diligent, demanding work lie between these two conditions.

What happens next brings the individual to an inner crossroad. If the insight dawns that this is still the way to be followed, the student's expectations are adjusted to a realistic level that leads to gradual degrees of progress. The other response is severe disappointment or disillusionment, and the person drifts away from what now becomes an unpleasant burden.

Now it should be pointed out that some schools of thought posit that negativity, including evil itself, is all a state of mind.

According to this viewpoint, by simply putting all of life in a positive light, we rise above a consciousness of toil and trouble. But this amounts to a Pollyana attitude. The difficulty with this determinedly optimistic outlook is that it ignores the heart of the way blazed by the Christ—the encounter with Satan and the crucifixion experience involving the total crossing out of the self in surrender to God. It is against this background that all of our challenges and encounters with our personalities arise. These confrontations pervade all of our circumstances, all of our choices, and especially all of our inferior qualities that lie deeply rooted in our human nature.

This is not to say that a positive outlook is naive or unwise. Quite the contrary, it is by far the better of alternatives. What it means is that such an optimistic viewpoint needs to be tempered with an insightful and resilient realism that can lead to actual growth and transformation.

At this point, enter the Angels! From the human standpoint it may be difficult to fathom their work and their ways. Keep in mind that they are selfless, untiring servers—a quality rarely observed in those of us from the human kingdom. They are immune to high-flying hopes or dark disappointments. They are absolutely steadfast in their service, as well as infinitely patient with us. They are also totally honest and sincere.

The Work and the Way of an Angel

An Angel will never misrepresent the facts of our failings or shortcomings. Yet their love for us exceeds by many-fold anything we can ever know among our human kind. They correct us in ingenious ways, standing with us, no matter our ignorance, indifference, or contrariness.

To most of us, what could be more boring than observing the passage of the hours of a fellow human through a typical day? Yet a Guardian Angel joyfully embraces this task. She vigilantly awaits any opening we give her to rid ourselves of the hold of the personality or its instinctive entanglements.

One of a Guardian's more useful resources in this enterprise of self-conquest is the human conscience mentioned previously. This functions much like an early warning system, sounding the alarm when we put ourselves at risk. True, much of what goes by that name of "conscience" can be attributed to societal standards, parental expectations, or moral scruples. However, when we find ourselves wrestling with our conscience in a manner that amounts to rationalizing the truth or justifying an untruth, it is time to examine what we are about, and why. It is also time to come to centeredness and receptivity where the Angels are concerned—to listen with the inward ear, and offer them an open channel to clarify their instruction.

Much of what takes place with Angels is conveyed in the language of signs and symbols. This is a time-honored means of communication with God's world. The key to this language is intuition. For example, your eyes fall upon a certain object and in a flash you realize its meaning. It is well to prize such moments, for they are the handiwork of an Angel, most often our Guardian Angel.

A variation on this form of enlightenment occurs when we search out information for one purpose, only to come upon an unexpected finding of much greater significance — a kind of serendipity. How many times have any of us gone into the book stacks of a library in search of information on one topic only to stumble upon a treasure trove of information on a totally different subject of far greater value. Our Guardian often uses such opportunities to call important matters to our attention.

She is particularly helpful in locating lost articles or documents. This usually happens when we have searched everywhere, exhausting our own possibilities. At this point if we pause to reverently, trustingly ask her assistance, we are likely to be led to the lost object. Do not be surprised if the lost item turns up in the very place you first searched!

Synchronicity

There is another gateway through which Angels commune with us. It was first described by Carl Jung and plays a key role in leading us to enlightenment. This is the experience of *synchronicity*, the coming together of two events not normally associated or expected to occur together, and in such a way that discovering its significance is truth-revealing and often life-changing.

Examples abound in the lives of the awakened, for it is a favorite means of arresting our attention or opening our eyes to a truth. Illustrating this occurrence, in the movie *Ben Hur* there is a deeply moving scene, after this noble Jewish merchant is condemned to serve the rest of his life as a galley slave on a Roman warship. Enroute to the Mediterranean Sea, his company of prisoners passes through a small village at whose well they rest. Desperately thirsty, Ben Hur looks in vain for a drink of water intentionally denied him by his Roman guard when who should be there to offer him that drink but Jesus of Nazareth. Of course, it marked the beginning of a fateful relationship that was to transform his life.

What ordinary observation would attribute to an "accident" or "coincidence" turns out to be a divinely intended event fraught with opportunity and meaning.

Whenever we find ourselves presented with such unusual occurrences—perhaps not so dramatic but no less noteworthy—we should afford them our closest attention and study. It is often in this manner that our Guardian Angel introduces us to new individuals, new resources, or new circumstances that promise to make a difference in our lives.

Remembrance and Receptivity

It is of utmost importance to keep in touch with the Angel kingdom through remembrance. Stopping in the midst of a busy day to thank them and appreciate their reality, even if only for a moment, makes all the difference. It engages us with their frequencies of communication; it opens the gates of intuition.

This condition is aptly called *receptivity*. Let us consider this simple prayer of attunement that Flower often used herself to invite contact with Divine sources. Come to a quiet moment and with utter sincerity, trust, and holy expectancy, say:

> *Inner, higher worlds,*
> *Inner, higher worlds,*
> *Send forth Thy light to me.*

Feel the veils of outer preoccupation fall away as you pronounce these words. Relax and come to peace. Let the Presence of the Divine seep into your soul.

Then say:

> *May that word,*
> *That baptism of force,*
> *That needed experience,*
> *Be impressed upon me now.*

Pause again and feel your whole being made receptive and permeable to inner instruction. Give that a moment or two to sink in. Then, with joy and thanksgiving say:

> *I am purposed to act*
> *With reverence, respect, and loyalty*
> *For all that is revealed.*

The words in the final pronouncement underscore a vital attitude when interacting with God's World—that we do so, not casually, or out of curiosity, or even dutifully, but with reverence, respect, and loyalty. When addressing the Inner Worlds, what is crucial is our motives. It strikes through to the heart of our integrity that we realize a profound responsibility when we consciously seek God's help. So it is that whatever comes to us, having exercised this prayer, we are committed to its fulfillment.

This prayer begins for us a magnificent adventure of inner instruction. For the most part, it is an adventure of insights and promptings involving the little things of life. The Angels, who know us only too well, realize that it is these "minor details" that we are prone to neglect or gloss over. We take care of major duties or responsibilities because they are more visible and consequential to the world around us. It is the little things we do, those that so easily can be swept under the rug or simply ignored, that reveal our true character.

Thus, the great bulk of our growth — what a Guardian prizes to transform—lies in the fine print of our life's story and in the nagging little mundane details that so often trip us up when neglected.

There is more to the adventure than coming to terms with our unfinished business. There are discoveries to be realized. Take for example, how we see things. Human perception is an amazingly creative capacity. No one has said this better than William Blake when he wrote:

> *To see a world in a grain of sand,*
> *And a heaven in a wild flower.*

The range of possibilities of how we see things is extraordinary. This versatility leaves a wide open door for the Angels to refine our perceptive skills, most often by revealing to us what lies beyond the surface of our experience.

The word *illumination* aptly describes where this refinement leads. In the classic instance of this phenomenon, we have Saul on the road to Damascus who, in the twinkling of an eye, beholds the Christ and is transformed into Paul. On a smaller scale, and more typical, we suddenly realize that life is a precious opportunity, full of rich possibilities and revelations. Or in a reflective moment, we might see a valued quality in another person never noticed before, and with that insight the entire relationship changes. Paul's experience may be singular and unique, but certainly the other two awakenings are the handiwork of a Guardian Angel. When the foundation has been laid and the time is right, she becomes the catalyst who ushers in the new awareness.

Our Guardian is like a sculptor. She studies our features with infinite care, and when we turn at just the right angle that invites her craftsmanship, she chips off another bit of the coarseness beneath which lies our true beinghood.

Our Guardian does not choose the time, she always waits for our readiness and will for this refining. We humans, who relish taking credit for our gains, think we ourselves are the clever ones. The time must come when we will have the awareness and the greatheartedness to acknowledge that we acted not alone but in league with Angels.

Index

Your Own Angel Experience

(here is the space to note your own experiences with Angels)

Your Own Angel Experience

Your Own Angel Experience

Your Own Angel Experience